KU-024-452

615.39 MCC

Tralee General Hospital Library

ACC. No. ~~001010~~ 615.39
Class MCCD

~~001~~ 001016

This book must be returned not later than the last date stamped below.

FINES WILL BE RIGOROUSLY IMPOSED

London: The Stationery Office

KH00772

© Dr D B L McClelland 1999
Adapted with permission of the copyright holder
Applications for reproduction should be made to:
Dr D B L McClelland
Director SE Scotland Regional Transfusion and
Department of Transfusion Medicine
Royal Infirmary
Edinburgh EH3 9HB

ISBN 0 11 702698 0
Republic of Ireland Edition 1999

Published by The Stationery Office and available from:

The Publications Centre
(mail, telephone and fax orders only)
PO Box 276, London SW8 5DT
General enquiries 0044 (0)171 873 0011
Telephone orders 0044 (0)171 873 9090
Fax orders 0044 (0)171 873 8200

The Stationery Office Bookshops
123 Kingsway, London WC2B 6PQ
0044 (0)171 242 6393 Fax 0044 (0)171 242 6394
68-69 Bull Street, Birmingham B4 6AD
0044 (0)121 236 9696 Fax 0044 (0)121 236 9699
33 Wine Street, Bristol BS1 2BQ
0044 (0)117 926 4306 Fax 0044 (0)117 929 4515
9-21 Princess Street Manchester M60 8AS
0044 (0)161 834 7201 Fax 0044 (0)161 833 0634
16 Arthur Street, Belfast BT1 4GD
0044 (0)1232 238451 Fax 0044 (0)1232 235401
The Stationery Office Oriel Bookshop
The Friary, Cardiff CF1 4AA
0044 (0)1222 395548 Fax 0044 (0)1222 384347
71 Lothian Road, Edinburgh EH3 9AZ
0044 (0)131 228 4181 Fax 0044 (0)131 622 7017

The Stationery Office's Accredited Agents
(see Yellow Pages)

and through good booksellers

Contents

P/O NO:
ACCESSION NO: KH00772
SHELFMARK: 615.39/mcc

BANTRY GENERAL HOSPITAL LIBRARY 615.39 McC

Preface to the Republic of Ireland edition of the Handbook of Transfusion Medicine

The transfusion of blood or blood products is increasingly seen by the public and by the caring professions as a serious therapeutic intervention, not to be undertaken without a sound reason and a clearly favourable risk – benefit ratio. While this approach applies to all therapeutic activities, it is highlighted in the case of blood transfusion by the recent history where a therapeutic agent previously considered at best life-saving and at worst a benign tonic has become mainly associated instead with disease transmission and avoidable morbidity and mortality.

For the practicing clinician it has become essential to understand thoroughly the use of blood transfusion. This includes knowledge of the nature the products, their clinical indications, the limits of their usefulness, and the clinical manifestations of the associated adverse effects.

This handbook is intended to provide a source of information and reference for transfusion of blood and blood products in clinical practice in Ireland. It is intended to keep this as a source of up to date information, and that it should be regularly updated to reflect advances in clinical practice and feedback from users.

Comments on the handbook will be welcomed and taken into consideration in the preparation of future editions. They should be addressed to the National Medical Director, Blood Transfusion Service Board, 40 Mespil Road, Dublin 4, email nmd@btsb.ie, fax 01-660-3914.

William Murphy
National Medical Director, Blood Transfusion Service Board, Dublin.

DBL McClelland
Editor

Chapter 1

About this book

About this book

Audience

This book is for staff who are responsible for prescribing, supplying and administering blood products. Many people have an essential part in making sure that the right blood product is given to the right patient at the right time. They include:

- Medical staff who assess the patient and prescribe and order the product.
- Laboratory staff who receive the order and prepare the product, matching it to the patient's blood group where necessary.
- Transport and delivery personnel who deliver the product to the patient.
- Nurses, who have a critically important responsibility in carrying out the checks before the product is administered and observing the patient during and after the transfusion.

Evidence

Correctly used, blood and blood products can save life or provide many important benefits to patients. However the effectiveness of much of today's blood transfusion practice has not been rigorously proved by clinical trials. It is therefore not possible to give a complete, evidence based guideline for practice. We have tried to use existing evidence about effective treatment. Where good evidence is not available, the contents reflect our best effort to give a balanced view of current opinion about good clinical practice in transfusion.

It is important to emphasise that throughout the world, decisions about safe and effective practice have to take account of different local situations, for example epidemiology of infectious diseases, availability of intravenous fluids, and access to supplies of good quality blood products.

Key topics

Most of the problems with transfusion that cause delays and may put the patient at risk are caused by poor communication or failure to follow procedures that should be well documented and in which staff should be well trained. Common problems include:

- Prescribing blood products that are not required by the patient or are not the most suitable for the patient's needs.
- Incomplete or inaccurate completion of request forms or sample tube labels.
- Delays caused by a failure to communicate accurately when and where the blood is needed.
- Transfusion of blood products that were intended to be given to someone else (this *does* happen!)
- Failure to recognise and react effectively to evidence of adverse reactions that occur during transfusion.

Some rare complications of transfusion, such as the transmission of viral infections may only be recognisable many days, weeks, or even years after the blood product has been given. Clinical staff have the responsibility of recognising and reporting problems of this type to the supplier (usually the hospital transfusion department). It is the task of the producer (the Blood Transfusion Service or other manufacturer of the blood product) to ensure that the products supplied are as safe and as effective as possible, and that reported adverse events are effectively followed up.

Glossary of terms and abbreviations

Apheresis (Single Donor) Platelet Concentrate	Platelets prepared by apheresis of the donor
Apheresis (Single Donor) Plasma	Plasma prepared by apheresis of the donor
Artificial Colloid Solutions	Gelatins, dextrans, hydroxyethyl starch
Anti-D Immunoglobulin	Human IgG preparation containing a high level of antibody to the Rh D antigen

Autologous Transfusion	General term for several techniques e.g. – preoperative blood donation – perioperative isovolaemic haemodilution – salvage from operation site (intraoperative) – salvage from operation site (postoperative)
Blood Components	Whole blood, red cells, plasma, platelets, cryoprecipitate prepared in the Regional Transfusion Centre
Blood Products	Any therapeutic product derived from human whole blood or plasma donations
CJD	Creutzfeldt-Jakob Disease
CMV	Cytomegalovirus
Colloid Solutions (artificial colloids)	Gelatin; Dextran, starch preparations: table 11a, page 49.
Crystalloid Solutions	Saline, Ringer's lactate etc.
DIC	Disseminated intravascular coagulation
Epoietin	Approved name for recombinant human erythropoietin
FFP	Fresh frozen plasma. Plasma that is frozen within a specific time period after collection and stored in the frozen state until thawed for transfusion or crushed for fractionation.
GvHD	Graft versus host disease
HAV	Hepatitis A virus
HBV	Hepatitis B virus
HCV	Hepatitis C virus
HEV	Hepatitis E virus
HGV-C or GBV-C	Hepatitis G virus; a recently described virus of uncertain significance
HTLV I	Human T Cell Leukaemia virus type I
Human Parvovirus B19	A non-enveloped virus transmissible by blood products and potentially pathogenic in some groups of patients
International Normalised Ratio (INR)	A standardised method for reporting the prothrombin time

Kleihauer Test	Acid elution of blood film to allow counting of fetal cells in maternal blood
Massive Transfusion	Defined variously as replacement of 1 blood volume within 24 hours, transfusion of more than 20 units of red cell concentrate, or replacement of >50% of blood volume in 3 hours.
NANB Hepatitis	Non A Non B hepatitis: former operational term for the most common class of post-transfusion hepatitis. Now known to be largely due to Hepatitis C virus, and >80% eliminated by HCV screening of donations.
PCC	Prothrombin complex concentrate
Plasma Fractions	Partially or highly purified human plasma proteins prepared under pharmaceutical manufacturing conditions and generally licensed by the Irish Medicines Board
Recovered Plasma	Plasma prepared from individual donations of whole blood
Recovered ('Random Donor') Platelet Concentrate	Platelets prepared from individual donations of whole blood
Red Cells	The term is used for any red cell component unless otherwise stated
Rh D	The most immunogenic antigen of the Rhesus blood group system
Saline	Sodium chloride intravenous infusion 0.9%
TTP	Thrombotic thrombocytopenic purpura
Viral Inactivation	Additional manufacturing step in making blood products: validated to remove or substantially reduce infectivity for specified viruses. Some viruses may not be reliably inactivated by all the current methods.

Feedback

This edition of the handbook has been improved by many comments and criticisms received from users of the first and second editions. The production team depend on readers of this edition to help improve the next revision.

Please e-mail your comments, ideas and criticisms to the editor Brian McClelland@SNBTS1.SNBTS.SCOT.NHS.uk or fax to 44 131 5365352 or to W Murphy (e-mail nmd@btsb.ie; fax (353) 01 660 3914).

Authorship

The people who prepared and evaluated this handbook are listed below, with their contact details. If you need specialist advice, you may find it useful to contact one of them. We will do our best to give an answer to your questions – and to include the important points in the next edition of the handbook.

Additional comments were received from haematologists throughout the Republic of Ireland in the preparation of this edition.

Editor:

D B L McClelland
Director, Edinburgh & South East Scotland Blood Transfusion Service
Senior Lecturer, University of Edinburgh Medical School
41 Lauriston Place
Edinburgh EH3 9HB

Contributors:

J A J Barbara
Consultant in Microbiology to the
National Blood Service, England
North London Blood
Transfusion Centre
Colindale Avenue
London NW9 5BG

M Brennan
Consultant
North London Blood
Transfusion Centre
Colindale Avenue
London NW9 5BG

S C Davies
Professor of Haemoglobinopathies,
Imperial College,
Central Middlesex Hospital
Acton lane
Park Royal
London NW10 7NS

J Gillon
Consultant, Edinburgh & South East
Scotland
Blood Transfusion Service and
Senior Lecturer, University of
Edinburgh Medical School
41 Lauriston Place
Edinburgh EH3 9HB

S M Knowles
Consultant and Clinical Director
South Thames Blood Transfusion
Service
75 Cranmer Terrace
Tooting
London SW17 ORB

W G Murphy
National Medical Director
Blood Transfusion Service Board
40 Mespil Road, Dublin 4
Ireland

J A F Napier (retired)
Consultant and Medical Director
National Blood Transfusion Service
(Wales)
Rhydlafar
St. Fagans
Cardiff CF5 6XF

W H Ouwehand
Lecturer
Division of Transfusion Medicine
University of Cambridge and
Consultant
East Anglian Blood Centre
Long Road
Cambridge CB2 2PT

R R C Stewart
Inveresk Clinical Research Ltd.
Research Park
Heriot Watt University
Riccarton
Edinburgh EH14

A Todd
Consultant
Edinburgh & South East Scotland
Blood Transfusion Service &
Department of Transfusion Medicine
The Royal Infirmary
41 Lauriston Place
Edinburgh EH3 9HB

L M Williamson
Lecturer
Division of Transfusion Medicine
University of Cambridge and
Consultant
East Anglia Blood Centre
Long Road
Cambridge CB2 2PT

P L Yap
Consultant, Edinburgh & South East
Scotland
Blood Transfusion Service and
Senior Lecturer, University of
Edinburgh Medical School
The Royal Infirmary
41 Lauriston Place
Edinburgh EH3 9HB

Reviewers

F Ala (retired)
Director
West Midlands Regional Blood
Transfusion Centre
Vincent Drive
Edgbaston
Birmingham B15 2SG

J D Cash (retired)
Medical & Scientific Director for the
Scottish National Blood Transfusion
Service
and President of the Royal College
of Physicians of Edinburgh
9 Queen Street
Edinburgh EH2 1JQ

M Contreras
Chief Executive and Medical Director
North London Blood Transfusion
Centre
Colindale Avenue
London NW9 5BG

M Greaves
Professor of Haematology
University of Aberdeen
Department of Medicine and Therapeutics
Polwarth Building
Foresterhill
Aberdeen AB25 7A1

F Hill
Consultant
Department of Haematology
The Children's Hospital
Ladywood Middleway
Ladywood
Birmingham B16 8ET

J S Lilleyman
Professor of Paediatric Oncology
St. Bartholomew's Hospital
London EC1A 7BE

J A F Napier
Consultant and Medical Director
National Blood Transfusion Service
(Wales)
Rhydlafar
St. Fagans
Cardiff CF5 6XF

A H Waters (retired)
Editor
Transfusion Medicine Journal
& Professor, Department of
Haematology
St. Batholomew's Hospital
West Smithfield
London EC1A 7BE

J K Wood
Consultant
Department of Haematology
The Leicester Royal Infirmary
Leicester LE1 5 5WW

Acknowledgement.

Republic of Ireland Edition. This edition was reviewed in addition by Dr Joan O'Riordan, Consultant Haematologist, and Dr Emen Lawlor, Consultant Haematologist, Blood Transfusion Service Board, and by Ms Deirdre Gough, Transfusion Nurse Specialist, St James's Hospital, Dublin. Additional comments and assistance were provided by other colleagues in practice in Ireland, and these are gratefully acknowledged by the Editor.

The manuscript was prepared for publication by Mrs Irene McKechnie, Edinburgh & South East Scotland Blood Transfusion Service. The figures were prepared by Mr Michael McLaughlin and Mr Robert Clarkson, ESEBTS.

We thank many other colleagues who have commented on the text and assisted with references.

Local systems and procedures.

If you are not familiar with the local system for obtaining blood products, visit the blood bank. The clinical and the technical staff there will be able to explain the system. In addition medical staff at the Blood Centres will be very happy to be contacted for general information or to answer specific queries. There is no substitute for talking with the people who are working to help you care for your patients.

Blood ordering in an emergency.

Procedures for identification of the patient and labelling of tubes and forms must be strictly followed.

The blood bank should be informed as quickly as possible of the quantity of blood needed and the time it is needed. Special transport arrangements may be required.

In some situations the blood bank may advise the use of Group O blood, but usual practice in Ireland is to provide blood of the patient's ABO and Rh D group. This can usually be issued within 15 minutes of the blood bank receiving a patient's blood sample. Local arrangements vary. **If your job is likely to involve urgent blood ordering you must make yourself familiar with the local system.**

Unmatched Group O blood should only be requested and used when the patient's life would be at risk if there were *any* avoidable delay in giving blood. **Group O negative blood is almost always in short supply. If it is used when it is not absolutely necessary, the supply for other real emergencies will be depleted.**

Figure 1:   The blood transfusion process from donors to patients

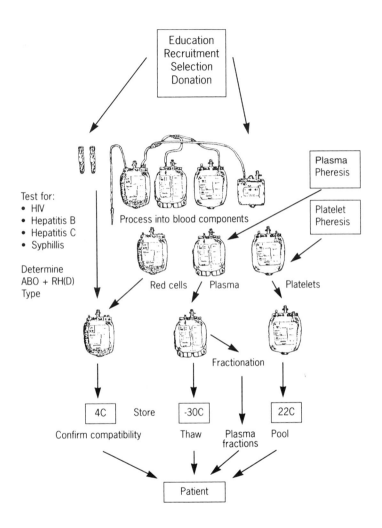

Education
Recruitment
Selection
Donation

Plasma
Pheresis

Test for:
• HIV
• Hepatitis B
• Hepatitis C
• Syphillis

Process into blood components

Platelet
Pheresis

Determine
ABO + RH(D)
Type

Red cells   Plasma   Platelets

Fractionation

4C   Store   -30C   22C

Confirm compatibility   Thaw   Plasma   Pool
                                 fractions

Patient

Names of blood products

In this book we have used the following convention.

– *Blood products* Any therapeutic substances prepared from human blood.

– *Blood components* Red cells
Fresh frozen plasma
Platelets
Cryoprecipitate
White cells
Progenitor cells collected from peripheral blood ('stem cells').

– *Plasma fractions* These are partially purified human plasma proteins made under pharmaceutical manufacturing conditions, including coagulation factors, immunoglobulins and albumin.

Names of other fluids

The following short terms are used in the text.

– *Crystalloid* Saline, Dextrose, Ringer's solution, etc.

– *Saline* Sodium chloride injection 0.9% BP.

– *Colloids* Dextran, modified fluid gelatin, hydroxyethyl starch.

The concept of blood component therapy

It is useful for the prescriber to understand a few basic facts about how blood is collected and processed because this affects the safety and availability of the products. *Figure 1* illustrates the processing of blood from donor to patient. Blood is a raw material from which a range of therapeutic products including platelet concentrate, red cell concentrate and fresh plasma are made. Large amounts of plasma are also needed for the production of plasma fractions such as albumin, coagulation factors and immunoglobulins. Plasma is obtained from whole blood donations as shown in the figure. Some is obtained by plasmapheresis.

Blood donors and blood donation testing

Donors can give 450 ml whole blood, generally up to 4 times per year Platelets, plasma and leucocytes can also be collected by cytapheresis. An apheresis platelet collection generally comprises a single platelet dose for an adult.

The medical selection of donors is intended to exclude anyone whose blood might harm the recipient, for example by transmitting infection, as well as to protect the donor from any risk. In Ireland every blood donation is tested for evidence of infection with Hepatitis B, Hepatitis C, HIV-1, HIV-2, HTLV I & II, and syphilis. In other countries, different tests for infection may also be needed, depending on the frequency of infection in the community. Each donation is tested to determine the blood group (ABO and Rh D).

Table 1: *Blood donors and donation*

- **Healthy persons aged 18-70 can give blood.**

    At each attendance donors complete a questionnaire or are interviewed to identify those
    - who could be harmed by donating, or
    - whose blood could harm a patient.

- **Donation may be**

    - Whole blood: up to 4 times per year
    - Plasma by apheresis: up to 15 l/yr or
    - Platelets by apheresis: up to 24 times/yr

Blood donations from relatives or friends ('directed' donation)

Blood provided by a patient's relatives or friends specifically for that patient is called 'directed' donation. This does not reduce the risk of virus transmission. Directed donations may on occasion be less safe since the donors may not be true volunteers and may have reasons for being reluctant to disclose information that should exclude them from donation.

There are occasional circumstances, such as neonatal alloimmune thrombocytopenia in which it may be safer to transfuse a mother's platelets to her baby. Other types of directed donation should be discouraged.

Irradiation

Donations from blood relatives have caused fatal graft versus host disease. Therefore if a patient has to receive blood from a relative, any cellular blood component *must* be irradiated.

Preparation of blood components

Blood is collected into sterile plastic packs which are centrifuged to separate red cells, platelets and plasma. (Figure 1). Plasma intended for direct transfusion as Fresh Frozen Plasma may be further processed to reduce the risk of viral transmission, for example by the addition of a photosensitive chemical and subsequent activation of the chemical by white light. Plasma may alternatively be further processed into plasma fractions.

Manufacture of plasma fractions

Plasma fractions are partially purified therapeutic preparations of plasma proteins. They are manufactured, in a large scale pharmaceutical process, from large volumes of plasma. Typically the plasma from up to 20,000 individual donations, about 5,000 kg of plasma, is processed by the addition of ethanol and exposure to varying temperature, pH and ionic strength conditions to precipitate different proteins. Further purification and virus inactivation steps are carried out. The final products are freeze dried powders or solutions.

Since plasma from any one of the individual donors who contribute to each batch of products could potentially introduce infectious organisms, careful screening of every donation is vital. Even with screening, some viruses could find their way into the pooled plasma, so the manufacturing processes include steps to inactivate any infectious agents which might escape detection.

Labels

Blood components carry labels applied by the Blood Centre that produced them and also by the hospital transfusion department. The Blood Centre labels contain the information that is important for staff who administer products and also allow the origins of the product to be traced. The label applied by the hospital transfusion department should contain information that uniquely identifies the patient for whom the component has been selected. *An essential step before administering any blood component is to make sure that the details on this label (usually called the 'compatibility label') match exactly with the identity of the patient (page 35). Figure 2 shows the main features of blood component labels.*

Figure 2: Blood component label.

Name of manufacturer, product licence number, type of plastic

Donation number

Correct testing, storage and administration of blood components make transfusion very safe but this cautionary note is a reminder that zero risk cannot be guaranteed

Blood group and Rhesus D type of red cells

Collection centre

Expiry date ("use before")

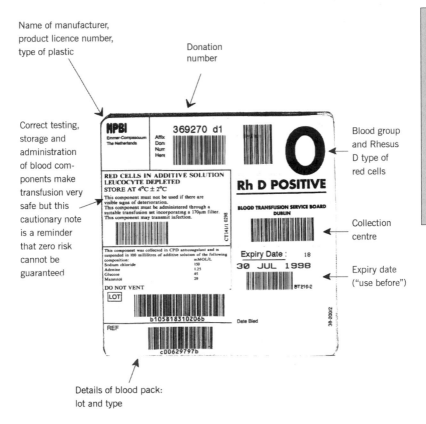

Details of blood pack: lot and type

Chapter 2

Blood products

Blood products

Essential Information

The tables that follow summarise important information about the use, storage and content of blood products. More information is available in the 'further reading' section, or from your supplier of blood products.

Table 2: *Blood products – Virological safety*

- All donations of whole blood, plasma and platelets are tested to exclude the following viruses transmissible by blood: Hepatitis B, Hepatitis C, HIV 1 and 2, HTLV I & II.

- Blood components may be subjected to further manufacturing procedures to reduce risk of virus transmission.

- These include:
  Virus inactivated plasma.
  Leucocyte depleted components (effective leucocyte filtration removes the risk of transmitting cytomegalovirus). During 1998 and 1999 routine leucocyte depletion for all cellular blood components will be introduced in Ireland by the Blood Transfusion Service.
  CMV antibody negative components (exclusion of components containing antibody removes the risk of transmitting CMV).

- Plasma Fractions are subjected to further manufacturing procedures to remove or reduce the risk of transmission of Hepatitis B, Hepatitis C, HIV and other viruses.

Table 3: Blood components – storage and administration

	Red cells (Additive) Whole Blood	Platelet Concentrate Recovered (Random Donor)	Platelet Concentrate Apheresis (Single Donor)	Fresh Frozen Plasma	Cryoprecipitate
Storage temperature	2 to 6C	At 20–24C on a special agitator rack		–30C	–30C
Shelf life	35 days	5 days	5 days	6–12 months	6–12 months
Longest time from leaving controlled storage to completing infusion	5 hours	Depends on preparation method: consult supplier		4 hours after thawing	4 hours after thawing
Compatibility testing requirement	Must be compatible with recipient's ABO and RhD type and clinically significant red cell antibodies	Preferably ABO compatible. Rhesus negative females under the age of 45 years should be given RhD negative platelets	Should be ABO compatible to avoid risk of haemolysis caused by donor Anti A or Anti B		

Points to Note:
Administration

- **Infuse through a blood administration set**
- **Record details of each blood component infusion in the patient's case record**
- **Follow local procedures or protocols for ordering and administering blood components**

Blood products

Table 5: Platelet products

unit	Platelets Recovered† (Random Donor)	Leucocyte Depleted† Apheresis Platelets	Apheresis (Single Donor)† Platelets	HLA Compatible† Apheresis Platelets	Crossmatched† Apheresis Platelets
*Volume	40-60 ml of plasma per donation	1 Donation — Check local product specification			
Content of platelets	At least 55×10^9 per donation	$>240 \times 10^9$			
Content of white cells	$<0.2 \times 10^9$/donation	$<5 \times 10^6$	$<0.8 \times 10^9$		
Points to Note Prescribing	Adult dose 4-6 donations containing $>240 \times 10^9$ platelets	Can help to reduce development of allo-antibodies to leucocyte antigens. An alternative to CMV-negative product	Contain sufficient volume of a single donor's plasma, to cause a risk of haemolysis if the donor has potent red cell antibodies. Donor should be ABO compatible — Adult dose: 1 donation	Donors are selected to match recipient for some HLA antigens. May be effective in patients who do not respond to platelets due to HLA antibodies	Donors are selected by a test for reaction with recipient's plasma. May be effective in patients who do not respond to platelets due to HLA antibodies

*Typical volumes are given.

†It is planned that all platelet products will be leucocyte depleted from 1999 onwards.

Table 6: *Fresh frozen plasma and cryoprecipitate*

	Recovered (Random Donor) FFP	Apheresis (Single Donor) FFP	Cryosupernatant Plasma	Cryoprecipitate
Unit	←——————————— 1 Donation ———————————→			
Volume ml	150–300 plasma containing anticoagulart solution	500–600 of plasma containing anticoagulant solution	150–250	10–20
	←——————— Check local product specification ———————→			
Content per 200 ml Unit				
Sodium mmol			35	
Glucose mmol			4	
Potassium mmol			1	
Citrate mmol			4	
Lactate mmol			1	
Hydrogen ion nmol			12	
Fibrinogen	2–5 mg/ml	2–5 mg/ml	Low	150–300 mg/pack
von Willebrand Factor	0.7 unit/ml		Low	80–120 u/pack
Factor VIIc	0.7 unit/ml	0.7 unit/ml	Low	80–120 u/pack
Other plasma proteins	←——————— As in slightly diluted plasma ———————→			
Added chemicals	←——————— Citrate Phosphate Dextrose Adenine ———————→			

Table 6: *Fresh frozen plasma and cryoprecipitate continued*

	Recovered (Random Donor) FFP	Apheresis (Single Donor) FFP	Cryosupernatant Plasma	Cryoprecipitate
Points to Note Prescribing	• Risk of volume overload • Occasional severe anaphylactic reactions, especially with rapid infusion rates • Infection risks are similar to those of other blood components • Contain normal levels of plasma immunoglobulins including red cell antibodies that can damage recipients' red cells • The dosage of FFP depends upon the clinical situation and underlying disorder but 12–15 ml/kg is a generally accepted starting dose. It is important to monitor the response both clinically and with measurement of prothrombin time (PT), partial thromboplastin time (PTT) or specific factor assays			Use virus inactivated products in preference whenever it is possible

Table 7: *Human plasma fractions*

	Human Albumin	Human Immunoglobulin	
		For intramuscular Use	*For Intravenous Use*
Unit	Typically 20g as 400 ml of 5% solution or 100 ml of 20% solution*	Varies with product and supplier	
Active constituents include	Human albumin	Human IgG – from a large pool of unselected donors – or from donors with high levels or anti Rh D or anti-viral antibodies	Human IgG – from a large pool of unselected donors
Other constituents include	Sodium 130–150 mmol/l Other plasma proteins Stabilizer (sodium caprylate)	Other immunoglobulins and other plasma proteins	Other immuno-globulins and other plasma proteins. Sucrose, pepsin
Main clinical uses	Hypoproteinaemic oedema with nephrotic syndrome (20%) Ascites in chronic liver disease (20%) Acute volume replacement (5%) in plasmapheresis – see page 42	Prophylaxis of specific virus infections such as hepatitis A, B, Varicella Zoster. Prevention of Anti Rh (D) sensitization in at risk mothers	Treatment of inherited and acquired deficiencies of antibody formation. Treatment of immunological disorders such as auto-immune thrombocytopenic purpura (AITP)
Points to Note: Prescribing	20% solution: hyperoncotic and expands plasma volume by more than the amount infused. 5% solution: use carefully if patient is at risk of sodium retention. For acute volume replacement, there is no evidence that 5% Albumin is superior to alternative fluids.	**See pages 69 + 70**	
Storage	At room temperature		

Clotting Factor Concentrates			
Factor VIII*	Factor IX	Prothrombin Complex Concentrate	Others Include
Typically 250–500 iu in each vial			Factor VII Antithrombin III Fibrin Sealant [Recombinant Factor VIII] [Recombinant Factor VIIa] FEIBA (Factor VIII inhibitor bypassing activity concentrate)
Factor VIII*	Factor IX	Factors II, IX, X. Some products contain Factor VII *almost completely superseded by recombinant factor VIIIC	
← **Other human plasma proteins** →			See supplier's information
Treatment of haemophilia A	Treatment of haemophilia B	Replacement of multiple clotting factor deficiencies. Rapid correction of oral anti-coagulant effect	See supplier's information

See Page 61

All these products should be used under the guidance of a specialist clinician

Usually at 4C but check manufacturer's information

Chapter 3

Procedures

Procedures

Information for patients

Explain the proposed transfusion treatment to the patient or relatives, and record in the case-notes that you have done so!

Patients or their relatives may be worried about the risks of transfusion. Some may wish to know more about the risks, about the need for transfusion and about alternatives such as autologous transfusion or drugs such as erythropoietin. Patients of the Jehovah's Witness faith are strictly banned by their religious beliefs from receiving blood components, but may be prepared to accept plasma fractions or alternative treatments.

Answers to most patient's questions should be found in this book. We have also included an outline of an information sheet for patients on page 98. You should check if your hospital has a leaflet of this type and if your patients receive it.

Recording the reason for transfusion.

Before blood products are administered, the reason for transfusion (which should usually comply with local or national guidelines) should be written in the patient's case-notes. **This is important. If the patient has a problem later on, that could be related to transfusion, the records should show *who* ordered the products, and *why*.**

Ordering red cell products

This section may seem to be very pedantic but experience everywhere shows that **dangerous or fatal transfusion errors are usually caused by failing to keep to the standard procedures.**

Acute **haemolytic** transfusion reactions are usually caused by transfusing red cells that are incompatible with the patient's ABO type. These reactions can be fatal. They usually result from errors made in identifying the patient when samples are being taken or when blood is being administered.

When ordering and giving blood products it is therefore essential to *follow the local procedures*. These should cover the steps outlined in Figure 3.

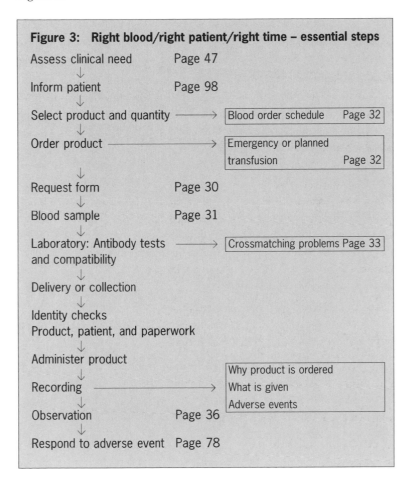

Figure 3: Right blood/right patient/right time – essential steps

Assess clinical need — Page 47
↓
Inform patient — Page 98
↓
Select product and quantity ──→ Blood order schedule — Page 32
↓
Order product ────────→ Emergency or planned transfusion — Page 32
↓
Request form — Page 30
↓
Blood sample — Page 31
↓
Laboratory: Antibody tests ──→ Crossmatching problems Page 33
and compatibility
↓
Delivery or collection
↓
Identity checks
Product, patient, and paperwork
↓
Administer product
↓
Recording ────────→ Why product is ordered / What is given / Adverse events
↓
Observation — Page 36
↓
Respond to adverse event — Page 78

Ordering blood in an emergency

This will often be done in the emergency admissions unit. There may be several unconscious patients who need blood quickly. Often many staff are involved. It is very easy to make mistakes, *so procedures must be clear, and simple and everyone must know them.*

- For each patient, the crossmatch sample tube and the blood request form must be clearly labelled with the EMERGENCY ADMISSION NUMBER. **Check local procedures!** Use the patient's name only if you are sure you have correct information.

- If you have to send another request for the same patient within a short period, use the same identifiers that you used on the first request so the hospital transfusion department staff know they are dealing with the same patient!

- It may help if one person takes charge of ordering blood especially if several patients are involved at the same time; that person should communicate with the hospital transfusion department.

- Tell the hospital transfusion department how quickly the blood is needed for each patient. This allows the laboratory to provide the blood when it is needed.

- Make sure that both you and the hospital transfusion department staff know

  - *who* is going to bring the blood to the patient
  - *where* the patient will be. For example if your patient is just about to be transferred for a CAT scan in another part of the hospital, make sure the blood will be delivered to the CAT scan room!

- The hospital transfusion department may send Group O Rhesus negative blood, especially if there is a risk of mistakes in patient identification. During an acute emergency, this may be the safest way to avoid a mismatched transfusion.

Prescribing blood products

It is the doctor's responsibility to prescribe blood products specifying the quantity to be given, duration of infusion and any other special precautions.

Request forms

- The blood request form should be clearly and accurately completed with the patient's family name, given name, date of birth and hospital number.

- Patients who at the time of admission cannot be reliably identified *must* be given an identity band with a unique number. This number

Procedures

must be used to identify this patient until full and correct details are available and are properly communicated to the hospital transfusion department.

- The quantity of the blood component required and the time at which it is needed should be written on the request form. The timing of blood ordering for planned procedures should comply with local rules, and the quantity requested for elective surgical patients should be guided by the local surgical blood ordering schedule.
- All the details requested on the form should be completed. It should be signed by the clinician with his or her name in *legible* capitals.

Blood samples for compatibility testing

In some hospitals the responsibility for taking samples from conscious patients is delegated to phlebotomists. They should be specifically trained for this work.

- At the time of taking the sample the conscious patient must be asked to state his/her given name, family name, and date of birth.
- This information must be checked against the patient's identification bracelet to make sure that the details entered on the request form are identical.
- The blood sample should be taken according to the hospital laboratory manual and the correct sample tube must be used (for adults, usually 10 ml, no anticoagulant).
- **The sample tubes must be accurately** *labelled at the patient's bedside at the time the blood sample is being taken.* **Sample containers must not be pre-labelled before the specimen is obtained because of the risk of putting the patient's blood into the wrong tubes.**
- In the case of unconscious patients a medical practitioner (or a specially trained and designated registered nurse per local protocol) should complete the request form and take the sample.

The hospital transfusion department staff are acting correctly if they refuse to accept a request for compatibility testing when either the request form or the sample is inadequately identified. At least 5% of samples arrive with labelling or form filling errors. This wastes time for all concerned and can contribute to serious errors.

Blood ordering for planned procedures.

- It is extremely important to check your local procedures in this regard. -

Blood ordering schedule or tariff (sometimes referred to as MSBOS: Maximum Surgical Blood Ordering Schedule)

The blood order for a planned procedure should reflect the clinical team's actual blood use for the particular operation. Many operations very rarely need blood component transfusion so there is no need to crossmatch blood as a routine.

The type and screen procedure should be used for procedures where red cell transfusion is only rarely required.

For procedures that often need red cell transfusion, the standard blood order should be based on the actual use of blood for patients who have recently undergone that operation, not taking account of the occasional patient who has unusually severe blood loss.

- **Type and screen, (also called 'group and hold' or 'group and save').** In the laboratory, the patient's ABO and Rh D type are determined and the patient's serum is screened for IgG antibodies that can damage red blood cells at 37°C. The patient's serum sample is then held in the laboratory, usually for 7 days. If red cells are required within this period they can be provided safely for the patient after a further rapid test to exclude ABO incompatibility. Using this method the hospital transfusion department will usually need about 15 minutes to have blood ready for issue to the patient.

  With this approach there is no need to hold units of blood as an 'insurance' for a patient who is unlikely to need them. As a result we can make better use of the donated red cells.

- **Red cell compatibility testing (crossmatching).** In addition to the group and screen, the patient's serum sample is usually tested by the hospital transfusion department for compatibility with the red cells of the units of blood to be transfused. Compatible units of blood are then labelled specifically for the patient and can be kept available for immediate release. The laboratory will usually reserve these units only for 48 hours (72 hours in some hospitals) after the time for which they were requested.

Where a patient needs further red cell transfusion and has had a recent red cell transfusion (completed more than 24 hours ago) a fresh sample should be sent for crossmatching. Red cell antibodies may appear very rapidly as a result of the immunological stimulus given by transfused donor red cells.

Crossmatching problems

When the patient's sample is found to contain a clinically significant red cell antibody further tests are needed to identify the antibody so that red cell units of a suitable blood type can be provided. The laboratory may well ask for another blood sample from the patient.

Every effort will be made by the transfusion department to provide blood that is compatible to avoid the risks of haemolytic transfusion reaction or of stimulating the patient's antibody to a high level. These tests may be complicated, and can cause considerable delay in providing red cells.

When this occurs, non urgent transfusions and surgery should be delayed until suitable red cell units are found, to avoid risks to the patient.

However, when a patient needs transfusion urgently and it is difficult to find compatible red cell units the doctor responsible for the transfusion department should be asked to advise on the risk of a life-threatening reaction if a red cell unit is given that is not fully compatible. *This risk must be balanced with the risk of delaying transfusion when a patient's life may be placed at risk from blood loss that urgently requires restoring the oxygen carrying capacity of the patient's blood.*

Storage, release and collection of red cells for transfusion

Red cells must be stored in a special, designated refrigerator. It is the responsibility of the hospital transfusion department to maintain these refrigerators and to specify the procedures to be followed when removing red cell units from them.

Crossmatched units of blood may be held within the hospital transfusion department or delivered to another blood refrigerator. In either case, the written procedure for removing red cell units for a patient should state:

- Who is authorised to collect red cell units from the refrigerator.
- The details that must be checked against the labels of the units being collected.
- The record that must be made of collection (and return) of the units, including:
  - the identity of the patient for whom blood is collected
  - the unique number of the red cell pack (Fig 2)
  - the time of collection
  - the name of person collecting the unit
  - the time of returning units to the refrigerator if they are not transfused.

Crossmatched red cell units will be collected by the transfusion laboratory if they have not been used within 48 hours of the time for which they were originally requested. *They must be kept in the blood refrigerator except when actually being transfused.*

Administering blood products

The procedures for infusing blood components should be defined by the hospital transfusion department with the medical and nursing staff. *The written procedures should be available to all staff who have to administer transfusions.* Responsibility for ensuring that the procedures are kept up to date and available, and for staff training must be defined by the hospital's management.

Identity checks

Follow local procedures for the checks to be undertaken and the staff who may perform them. The checking must involve two people, one of whom should be a registered nurse or doctor.

The hospital transfusion department should provide with the red cell units a compatibility report stating the patient's full identity, the patient's ABO and Rh D group and the unique donation number and group of each unit which has been supplied.

The compatibility label on each unit should show:
- Family name of patient
- Given name
- Date of birth and hospital number
- Patient's ABO and Rh D group
- Unique donation number
- Date and time for which blood is requested.

Occasionally red cells will be supplied that are of a different ABO group from the patient's but that are compatible - e.g. red cells of Group A are safe for a patient of Group AB. In this event (usually due to shortage of a particular group) the hospital transfusion department should inform the clinician responsible and also record the fact on the document that accompanies the blood units. Before starting the infusion, check that there are NO discrepancies between:

- Information on the patient's identity band, the compatibility label, and the compatibility report. Patients who can communicate should be asked to state their identity.
- The ABO and Rh D group on the blood pack, on the compatibility label and in the compatibility report.
- The donation number given on the blood pack, on the compatibility label and on the compatibility report.

If any discrepancies are found, the unit must not be transfused. If there is any suspicion that the contents of the pack appear abnormal (e.g. evidence of leakage, unusual colour or signs of haemolysis) the unit must not be transfused and the hospital transfusion department must be informed immediately.

Always check that:

- The expiry date on the blood pack has not been passed.
- There is no sign of leakage from the pack.

Procedures

Record keeping

The person administering a blood product must enter in the casenotes the number and blood group of the unit, the type of blood component, and the time at which the transfusion commenced. They must sign to indicate that the pre-administration checks have been performed. This document is part of the patient's permanent record.

Observe the patient

The following should be observed and recorded.

- Baseline pre-transfusion observation of pulse, blood pressure and temperature.
- Periodic check of pulse and temperature throughout the transfusion. This should be more frequent if there are unexpected symptoms or signs.
- Repeat observation of pulse, blood pressure and temperature at the end of the transfusion.
- Recording of the patient's fluid balance throughout the transfusion episode.

Observe the patient specially carefully during the first 15 minutes of the transfusion. If the patient starts to complain of pain at or near the transfusion site, distress, or loin pain, it can be the first indication of a transfusion reaction.

Clinical features and management of acute transfusion reactions are in Chapter 5.

Time limits for infusion

There is a risk of bacterial proliferation when blood components are kept at ambient temperature. For this reason a blood component transfusion must be started within 30 minutes of removing the pack from refrigeration and be completed within 5 hours. See Table 3 for other blood components.

Blood administration sets

For red cells, plasma and cryoprecipitate

Blood must be infused through a giving set containing an integral 170 micron filter. The set must be changed at least 12 hourly during blood component infusion.

For platelets

A fresh blood administration set or platelet transfusion set, primed with saline should be used to infuse platelets.

For small children

Special paediatric sets should be used.

Filtration of red cells and platelets

Microaggregate filters

There is no evidence from controlled trials that these offer clinical benefit. Common, but unproven indications are for massively transfused patients, transfusion for multiple trauma, and during cardiopulmonary bypass.

Leucocyte depleting filters

The use of red cell and platelet filters that reduce the level of leucocytes in transfusions varies from country to country; in Ireland routine leucocyte depletion during the processing of components at the Blood Centres is being introduced as a standard. The use of this technology reduces the immunogenicity of transfusions, particularly in relation to development of HLA antibodies that may contribute to platelet refractoriness; other benefits also accrue including prevention of transmission of cytomegalovirus by transfusion, diminished incidence of febrile transfusion reactions, and the possibility that prion disease transmission may be reduced.

Blood warmers

There is no evidence that warming blood is beneficial to the patient when infusion is slow. At infusion rates greater than 100 ml/minute case reports suggest that cold blood could cause cardiac arrest. Keeping the patient warm is probably more important than warming the infused blood.

Use of a blood warmer is advised for adults receiving infusion of blood at rates greater than 50 ml/kg/hour, for children receiving volumes greater than 15 ml/kg/hour and for infants undergoing exchange transfusions. A blood warmer is also indicated when transfusing a patient who has clinically significant cold agglutinins.

Blood warmers can be dangerous if they malfunction. They must have a visible thermometer and an audible warning and be properly maintained. Red cells and plasma exposed to temperatures over 40°C may cause severe transfusion reactions. Blood products must NOT be warmed by improvisations such as putting the pack into hot water, in a microwave, or on a radiator.

Do not add other pharmaceuticals to blood products

No other infusion solutions or drugs should be added to any blood component. They may contain additives such as calcium which can cause citrated blood to clot. Dextrose solution (5%) can lyse red cells. Drugs should never be added to any blood product. If there is an adverse reaction it may be impossible to determine if this is due to the blood, to the medication which has been added or to an interaction of the two.

If a crystalloid or colloid solution has to be given at the same time as blood components it should normally be given through a separate IV line.

Adverse reactions

Any adverse reaction thought to be related to the transfusion should be assessed as described in Chapter 5 and the clinical details and actions taken should be recorded in the case-notes.

Autologous transfusion

In some situations a patient can be transfused with their own blood that has been collected and stored in advance of a planned operation. There are theoretical advantages in this way of reducing the risk of immunological incompatibility or transmission of some infectious agents. There are detailed guidelines available for carrying out this procedure. *(Further reading).*

Red cells can be stored for up to 5 weeks using standard hospital transfusion department conditions. Medical selection must ensure that patients are fit for this procedure. Suitable patients can 'lay down' 2-4 units of blood pre-operatively. The blood must be tested, labelled and stored to the same standard as donor blood. Before transfusion, autologous blood units must be ABO and Rh D grouped and compatibility checked to avoid the consequences of any possible clerical errors. These 'autologous' donations should **not** be transfused to anyone other than the patient who provided the donation.

There are important practical limits to the application of pre-deposit auto-transfusion

- Not all patients are fit enough or live near enough to hospital to have 450 ml blood withdrawn several times before a planned operation.
- Auto-transfusion does not reduce the risk of bacterial infection hazards that may result from collection or storage problems. Nor does it reduce the risk of procedural errors that can cause ABO incompatible transfusion.
- Autologous units will often be left unused unless collection is restricted to patients undergoing operations that are very likely to involve a need for transfusion.
- Some patients will need donor blood *in addition* to their autologous units.
- Although pre-donation appears safe, there has been no systematic assessment of the risks.
- The cost of the procedure is reported to be high in relation to the gains in patient safety.
- There is new evidence that potentially dangerous mistakes occur quite frequently.

Certain categories, such as young fit individuals requiring elective major surgery with inevitable blood losses are likely to benefit most from pre-deposit autologous transfusion.

Patients must be carefully informed about the procedure, especially the possibility that they may receive donor blood (see page ??).

Immediate pre-operative bleeding and isovolemic haemodilution

This procedure may be useful in cardiothoracic surgery and other major procedures such as orthopaedic operations in young people. Immediately before operation, after induction of anaesthesia, blood is withdrawn with fluid replacement and stored in the operating theatre. After surgery, the patient's blood can be reinfused. This procedure allows the patient's haematocrit to be reduced to a level selected for optimal capillary perfusion, reduces red cell losses during surgery, and provides fresh autologous blood for reinfusion when needed.

Intra-operative blood salvage

During surgery blood shed into the operative field can be collected by suction, mixed with anticoagulant (unnecessary if the patient is heparinised) and reinfused through a filter. Using special equipment, the red cells can be washed before reinfusion. Because of concern about the risk of contamination, cell salvage is not advised in the presence of systemic sepsis, bacterial contamination of the operation field, or malignant disease.

Long term blood storage of autologous blood

Red cells can be stored for long periods at very low temperatures. Cryo-preservation is expensive. It should be reserved for patients with rare blood groups or with red cell antibodies that make it very difficult to find compatible donor blood.

Therapeutic apheresis

Therapeutic apheresis is the removal of blood or a blood component to benefit the patient's condition. The simplest procedure is therapeutic venesection in which whole blood (200-450 ml) is periodically withdrawn. This is indicated for some patients with haemochromatosis and polycythaemia. More commonly, cells or plasma are selectively removed using a cell separator. Methods for selective removal of plasma constituents (e.g. cholesterol, autoantibodies) are still at the experimental stage of development.

Good venous access is essential as a rapid blood flow is required for processing. Some machines can operate using a single vein but usually separate cannulae are required for blood withdrawal and return.

Plasma exchange

Therapeutic plasma exchange combined with other medical treatment contributes effectively to management of conditions shown in Table 8.

Table 8: *Indications for therapeutic plasma exchange (plasmapheresis)*

- Hyperviscosity syndromes e.g. myeloma, Waldenström's macroglobulinaemia

- Rapidly progressive glomerulo-nephritis e.g. Wegener's granulomatosis

- Goodpasture's syndrome

- Guillain-Barré syndrome

- Familial hypercholesterolaemia

- Thrombotic thrombocytopenic purpura

- Severe acquired Protein S deficiency usually seen in the post chicken pox setting

- Severe acquired Protein C deficiency usually seen in the setting of meningococcal infection. Protein C concentrate when available and intensive supportive management are also required

---

Plasma exchange has been used in many other conditions such as myasthenia gravis, pemphigus, SLE, other autoimmune disorders and in maternal Rh D sensitisation during pregnancy. Its effectiveness has not been proved in these conditions and in many cases objective monitoring is difficult. The potential risk and the high cost of plasmapheresis should be taken into account before using it in these conditions.

The replacement fluid for plasma exchange is usually 5% albumin, saline or a mixture of these. FFP may rarely be needed to correct a deficiency of coagulation factors at the end of a plasma exchange.

Thrombotic thrombocytopenic purpura

This rare and serious condition often responds to infusion of fresh frozen plasma (FFP), or of cryosupernatant plasma. Because large volumes of plasma may have to be given over a long period, plasma exchange, using plasma to replace the patient's plasma, is often used. **Plasma should only be used as exchange fluid in this specific indication, because of the associated risks of virus transmission and acute anaphylactic reaction.**

Cytapheresis (removal of blood cells)

Leucapheresis may help to alleviate symptoms and signs caused by very high cell counts in leukaemic patients (usually chronic granulocytic leukaemia) until chemotherapy takes effect. Plateletpheresis is occasionally used in patients with very high platelet counts causing bleeding or thrombosis. Erythrocytapheresis (red cell exchange) is occasionally needed in the management of malaria, sickle-cell crisis, polycythaemia or following a transfusion error in which Rh D positive blood is given to an Rh D negative female of child-bearing age.

Table 9: Complications of therapeutic apheresis

- Anaphylactic reactions to fresh frozen plasma
- Volume overload
- Hypovolaemia
- Air embolism
- Haemolysis
- Extracorporeal clotting
- Citrate toxicity
- Coagulopathy
- Vasovagal attacks

Progenitor cell (stem cell) collection by apheresis

Progenitor cells (autologous or allogeneic) can be collected from the peripheral blood by apheresis. This procedure is an effective alternative to the aspiration of bone marrow, and avoids the need for the patient or donor to have a general anaesthetic.

This procedure must be carried out by a specialist team, because the preparation of the patient, the cell collection, and the laboratory procedures to process, store and prepare the patient's cells for reinfusion must be very carefully planned and coordinated. There are detailed clinical guidelines available.

Procedures

Chapter 4

Clinical applications of blood products

Clinical applications of blood products

Principles

The following section deals with clinical situations that often involve the use of one or more blood products. Some general principles that apply to most clinical decisions about transfusion are given in Table 10.

Table 10:   *Minimise the need for donor blood products*

- Transfusion carries risks; some of these are specifically due to the use of allogeneic blood (i.e. blood from another person).

- Good clinical practice requires that blood products should be prescribed only when the benefit to the patient is likely to outweigh any risk.

- Prescribing decisions should be based on the best available clinical guidelines, modified according to individual patient needs. The rationale for prescribing should be part of the patient's record.

- For some patients in some clinical situations it may be safer to use the patient's own blood (autologous transfusion).

- 'Wastage' of a patient's blood can be minimised in many ways that can reduce the need for transfusion:
  - Minimise blood taken for laboratory use.
  - Use the best methods to minimise blood loss during surgery.
  - Salvage and reinfuse surgical blood losses during procedures where this is appropriate.
  - Use alternative approaches e.g. desmopressin, Aprotinin, Erythropoietin.
  - Stop anti-coagulants and anti-platelet drugs before planned surgery where it is safe to do so.
  - Use non-blood fluids for resuscitation.

- Transfuse to meet clinical need rather than responding to a laboratory result.

Perioperative red cell transfusion

When should red cell transfusion be given?

In the past surgeons and anaesthetists have often used the rule of thumb that a patient whose haemoglobin level has fallen below 10 g/dl (haematocrit <30%) needs red cell transfusion. There is no clinical evidence to support this generalisation. Some patients tolerate profound haemodilution during surgery without morbidity attributable to lack of red cells. Clinical studies do not support the general application of the '10g/30%' rule. However, in some older or 'fragile' patients, especially with cardiovascular disease, moderate haemodilution may contribute to myocardial ischaemia.

Conservative use of red cell replacement is appropriate in fit patients, especially the young, who are usually very tolerant of haemodilution, and for whom long term complications of avoidable transfusion are likely to be more important. (Table 11).

There is however little to commend the aggressive avoidance of red cell transfusion in elderly patients. Evidence of cardiovascular and respiratory disease should lead to caution in allowing haemoglobin to fall to a low level. In all patients with substantial blood loss, priority should be given to maintaining circulatory volume by giving adequate fluids and to maintaining oxygen supply.

Transfusion management of acute blood loss

This section refers to situations where rapid infusion of substantial volumes of fluid together with red cell replacement is likely to be required over a few hours, as a result of major bleeding.

Table 11: *Principles of transfusion management of acute blood loss*

Insert a large IV cannula, obtain blood samples, and first infuse crystalloid as rapidly as possible until an acceptable systolic blood pressure is restored.

- Restore circulating fluid volume to correct hypoperfusion.

- Achieve surgical control of bleeding.

- Maintain adequate blood oxygen transport capacity.

- Request early coagulation screen. The results may help to guide blood component therapy should bleeding persist after attempted surgical haemostasis.

% Loss of Blood Volume	Equivalent Adult Fluid Volume	Replacement Fluid
<20%	Up to 1 litre	– Crystalloid (eg 0.9% saline)
>20%	More than 1 litre	– Red Cells
		– Fluid: Crystalloid and/ or colloid

Notes:

1 To estimate blood volume: = 70 ml/kg in adults: 80 ml/kg in infants.

2 See Table 13, p55 for clinical features.

3 If bleeding continues after attempted surgical haemostasis and when coagulation tests or platelet count are abnormal, platelets, FFP or cryoprecipate or combinations of those may be needed: the dose should be estimated and the effect monitored by clinical evidence of reduced bleeding, coagulation screen and platelet count.

4 Clinical trials in humans have not demonstrated that albumin solutions or colloids are superior to crystalloids for resuscitation, but much larger volumes of crystalloids are required. A meta-analysis of published trials (1998) indicated that albumin is associated with poorer outcome.

5 Dextran and HES (Table 11a) should be limited to 1.5 litre per 24 hours in an adult (according to manufacturers' data sheets).

6 Avoid saline in patients with severe liver disease for whom sodium overload is a special risk. Also take care with 4.5% albumin in these patients for the same reason.

7 Clinical observations that should be routinely monitored and recorded throughout the management of an episode of bleeding are pulse rate, systolic BP, pulse pressure, urine output (catheter). CVP, arterial line and pulmonary artery catheter may also be required.

8 The type of crystalloid or colloid to be used and the source of supply should be specified in local protocols.

Table 11a: *Non plasma colloid volume expanders*

Product	Source	Concentration of solution	Average Mol. wt.	Intravascular persistence	Approximate frequency of severe acute reactions
Modified Fluid Gelatin	Heat-degraded cattle bone gelatin	3-4%	35,000	50% of infused volume persists 4-5 hours	1 in 10,000 infusions
Hydroxy-ethyl starch (HES)	Maize starch, chemically modified	6%	450,000 or 265,000	Similar to or longer than Dextran 70	1 in 20,000 infusions
Dextran 70	Hydrolysed Starch	6%	70,000	50% of infused volume persists 24 hours	1 in 10,000 infusions
Dextran 40	Hydrolysed Starch	10%	40,000	Shorter than Dextran 70	1 in 50,000 infusions

Obstetric haemorrhage

Haemorrhage remains an important cause of maternal mortality. The bleeding may be unpredicted and massive. The patient's life may depend on a fast effective response from the obstetric team, with the support of the hospital transfusion department.

A guideline for transfusion in obstetric bleeding has been published. *(See Further reading)*. Its main features are given in table 12.

Each obstetric unit should have a current protocol for major bleeding incidents and staff should be familiar with it.

Clinical applications of blood products

> **Table 12:** *Transfusion in obstetric bleeding*
>
> - Summon the extra staff required, (obstetrician, midwives, nurses and anaesthetist). Set up at least two I.V. lines (if possible, not less than 14 gauge). Use a compression cuff on the infusion pack and monitor central venous pressure (CVP) and arterial pressure. At the same time take blood for compatibility and coagulation screen. Typically a minimum of six units of red cells should be ordered. Alert your hospital blood bank. Make sure porters are available at short notice.
> - Fluid and Red Cell Replacement - page 48.
> - **Proper communication with the blood bank is vital: make sure they kow this is a real emergency.** If the blood bank is informed of the urgency, ABO and RhD compatible blood can usually be made available rapidly after receipt of the sample.
> - If red cell loss is life-threatening, uncrossmatched Group O Rh-negative red cells should be used if this is the fastest available source of red cells.
> - Regular haemoglobin or haematocrit assessment helps to control blood and fluid therapy, *but restoration of normovolaemia is the first priority.*
> - Coagulation screens should be performed to help detect haemostatic failure (usually due to DIC) and to help guide the use of blood components.
> - Patients with major haemorrhage require effective monitoring of pulse rate, blood pressure, CVP, blood gases and acid-base status. An indwelling urinary catheter should be inserted and urine output monitored. Dedicated care by the midwifery, nursing and medical staff is vital. Transfer to ITU or HDU should be considered *early.*

Transfusion support of major bleeding problems

Acquired haemostatic problems

Normal haemostasis involves pro-coagulant proteins (the coagulation cascade), the platelets, the fibrinolytic system, and the blood vessel wall. Acquired haemostatic disorders arise frequently in hospital practice. Blood component therapy is often required. Prescribing should be based on correct interpretation of clinical features and laboratory tests.

Haemostatic failure can be triggered by hypovolaemia, tissue damage, hypoxia and sepsis. Disseminated intravascular coagulation

(DIC) refers to a spectrum of haemostatic problems that may be seen in such conditions. Activation of the coagulation and fibrinolytic systems leads to deficiencies of coagulation proteins, fibrinogen, and platelets. The clinical presentation can range from major bleeding with or without thrombotic complications to a compensated state detectable only on laboratory testing.

Treatment should focus on correcting the cause of DIC. Replacement with blood products is indicated when there is bleeding with acute DIC. Platelets, fresh frozen plasma, and cryoprecipitate should be given to correct thrombocytopenia and clotting factor deficiencies. Control of bleeding is the goal; laboratory test results help to select the blood products that may be effective and to monitor the doses needed.

Neonates, patients with marrow disorders or liver disease and patients taking anticoagulants, aspirin or other non steroidal anti-inflammatory drugs are more likely to develop haemostatic problems because their platelet function is impaired and/or their haemostatic factor production is reduced. Where possible, seek advice from the hospital haematology or transfusion department physicians when managing these problems.

Blood component replacement

Dilution effect

When there is no pre-existing haemostasis problem, replacement of up to 1 blood volume (8-10 units of blood in an adult) with red cells and non-plasma fluids is unlikely to cause haemostatic problems due simply to dilution.

Platelets

In an adult, platelets should be given if there is severe microvascular bleeding with a platelet count below $50\text{-}100 \times 10^9/1$, (especially if more than 15 units of blood have been transfused) or if laboratory results suggest there is disseminated intravascular coagulation present.

There is no evidence that giving prophylactic platelets or plasma to patients undergoing large transfusions reduces the risk of microvascular bleeding. *Routine prophylactic use of these products for major surgery is not recommended.*

Fresh frozen plasma (FFP) and cryoprecipitate

FFP should be used only where there is microvascular bleeding with laboratory results that show abnormal coagulation. A dose of 15 ml/ kg is conventional (Table 6). If the fibrinogen level is below 1 g/l and DIC has been diagnosed with severe bleeding the fibrinogen level should be raised by giving cryoprecipitate, usually given in pools of ten units containing at least 2 to 3 gms of fibrinogen.

Laboratory tests of haemostasis

These can help to identify the need for blood components to control microvascular bleeding. The platelet count, Prothrombin Time (PT) or Activated Partial Thromboplastin Time (APTT) should be monitored during large transfusions to help guide replacement.

Other complications of large volume transfusions

The problems described below are rarely due to transfusion alone and cannot be avoided simply by attention to transfusion practice. However, transfusion should be managed so as to avoid making the problems worse.

Hypocalcaemia

The citrate anticoagulant in some blood components (Table 4) binds ionised calcium. This could lower plasma ionised calcium levels, but usually rapid liver metabolism of citrate prevents this. In neonates and patients who are hypothermic, the combined effects of hypocalcaemia and hyperkalaemia may be cardiotoxic. If there is ECG or clinical evidence of hypocalcaemia, 5 ml of 10% calcium gluconate (for an adult) should be given IV. If necessary the dose should be repeated till the ECG is normal. Note that red cells in additive solution contain only traces of citrate.

Hyperkalaemia

The plasma or additive solution in a unit of red cells or whole blood stored for 4-5 weeks may contain 5-12 mmol of potassium. In the presence of acidaemia and hypothermia this additional potassium can lead to cardiac arrest. This problem is best prevented by keeping the patient warm.

Hypothermia

Rapid transfusion of blood at 4°C can lower the core temperature by several degrees. The best safeguard is to keep the patient warm. A blood warmer should be used in adults receiving large volumes of blood at rates above 50 ml/kg/hr (in children above 15 ml/kg/hr).

Acid base disturbances

Despite the lactic acid content of transfused blood, [1-2 mmol/unit of red cells, 3-10 mmol/unit of whole blood] fluid resuscitation usually *improves* acidosis in a shocked patient. In practice, transfused citrate can contribute to metabolic *alkalosis* when large volumes of blood components are infused.

Adult respiratory distress syndrome

The risk is minimised if good perfusion and oxygenation are maintained and over-transfusion is avoided. The use of albumin solutions to maintain a plasma oncotic pressure >20 mmHg is often stated to be important but controlled studies have not proven any advantage of albumin solution over crystalloid fluids for resuscitation.

Avoidable haemostatic problems in the elective surgery patient

If a patient admitted for elective surgery or an invasive procedure is found to have thrombocytopenia or an abnormal coagulation screen (prolonged PT or APTT) the procedure should be postponed while the cause of the abnormality is identified. If a congenital bleeding disorder is found, the patient must be managed in conjunction with the haematology service/National Haemophilia Centre.

If the platelet count is below $80 \times 10^9/1$ before starting a procedure likely to cause significant blood loss, or below $100 \times 10^9/1$ where there may be bleeding in a critical site, e.g. CNS or eye, it must be investigated before starting the procedure.

Warfarin

Unless it is contra-indicated to do so, warfarin anticoagulation should be stopped before elective major surgery in time to allow the prothrombin time (INR) to approach normal. This should be guided by a local protocol for preoperative anticoagulant management.

Aspirin

A single dose of ½ tablet, 150 mg (or ½ junior aspirin, 75 mg), impairs platelet function for several days. Aspirin should be stopped at least 7 days before planned major surgery if it is safe to do so. When an aspirin-induced platelet defect contributes to abnormal bleeding, platelet transfusion is likely to be effective.

Transfusion for acute gastrointestinal bleeding

Gastrointestinal bleeding accounts for a substantial proportion of acute admissions to hospital and is associated with a significant mortality rate.

Blood replacement for patients with GI bleeding is summarised in Table 13. Special points in managing patients with bleeding from varices associated with chronic liver disease are given in Table 14.

Table 13: *Use of fluids and blood products in managing patients with acute gastrointestinal bleeding*
(based on extant guideline in a large unit specializing in the management of acute GI haemorrhage; not evidence based)

Severity	Clinical Features	IV Infusion	End Point

Severe	• History of collapse and/or
	
	• Shock
	  – systolic BP <100 mmHg
	  – pulse > 100/min
		• Replace fluid rapidly (Table 11)
		• Ensure red cells are available quickly; use local emergency transfusion protocol
		• Transfuse red cells according to clinical assessment and Hb/Hct (Table 11)
			Maintain urine output >0.5 ml/kg/ hr and systolic BP >100mHg
			Maintain haemoglobin above 9 g/dl

Significant	Resting pulse >100/min and/or haemoglobin less than 10 g/dl	Replacement fluid. Order compatible red cells (4 units)	Maintain haemoglobin above 9 g/dl
Trivial	Pulse and haemoglobin normal	• Maintain intravenous access until diagnosis is clear • Send patient sample for red cell group and antibody screen	

Table 14: Replacing gastrointestinal blood loss in patients with chronic liver disease

Features	Transfusion Mangement	End Points
• Bleeding is often but not always from oesophageal varices and is often severe. Other causes such as peptic ulcer are not uncommon and must be excluded	Insert one or two large bore cannulas. A central line may be indicated.	Systolic pressure >100 mmHg Haemoglobin 9 g/dl Urine output 0.5 ml/kg/hr.
• Bleeding from varices usually recurs if there is no intervention to control the varices or to reduce portal pressure. The prognosis depends on the severity of the liver disease.*	Ensure red cells are available quickly; use local emergency transfusion protocol: order 4-6 units.	CVP 0-5 mmHg (not higher)
• Hepatic failure may follow variceal bleeding, but usually recovers if bleeding can be stopped and recurrence prevented.	Crystalloids should be used carefully. Saline should be avoided as sodium retention is usual and leads to ascites.	
• Thrombocytopenia is usual. The platelet count may fall below 50 × 10^9/l. Provided the platelet count is above 50 × 10^9/l, bleeding is unlikely to be controlled or prevented by platelet transfusion.	Platelet transfusion is rarely needed. If there is continued bleeding with a platelet count below 50 × 10^9/l, platelet transfusion may be considered in an effort to control variceal bleeding.	Platelet count may show little increment following platelet transfusion in patients with splenomegaly.
• Normal (ie pre-bleed) systolic BP is often lower than in non-cirrhotic patients.		

Table 14: _Replacing gastrointestinal blood loss in patients with chronic liver disease continued_

Features	Transfusion Mangement	End Points
• Deficiency of coagulation factors is frequent.	Fresh frozen plasma is indicated only if there is documented coagulopathy. e.g. International Normalised Ratio (INR) >2.0.	Keep INR <2.0 if possible. Complete correction is rarely possible with FFP due to the large volume required.
• Giving red cells to try and raise Hb towards normal values may raise portal venous pressure, since blood volume is often increased. Over transfusion may contribute to rebleeding.		
• Provided blood volume is replaced and cardio-respiratory function previously adequate, a haemoglobin of 9 g/dl appears to be adequate.	Transfuse red cells to around 9 g/dl.	Coagulation factor concentrates have a risk of thrombo-genicity, in patients with liver disease. Use only with expert guidance.

Bleeding, especially if recurrent, is both intrinsically hazardous and is indicative of severe liver disease with a bad prognosis for the episode. A good outcome for the episode depends on overall management of infection, renal failure, ascites and encephalopathy.

Clinical applications of blood products

Warfarin (coumarin) anticoagulant overdose

Management should be guided by the principles in Table 15.

Clinical applications of blood products

Table 15: *Management of warfarin overdose*
–from Brit J Haematol 1998;101:374-378.

A Major haemorrhage

Give 5 mg vitamin K by slow intravenous infusion or by mouth and a prothrombin complex concentrate (PCC) either containing Factors II, VII, IX, X in a single preparation, or as two separate concentrates, one containing Factors II, IX, & X only and one containing Factor VII only. The dose should be based on 50 iu Factor IX or Factor VII per kg body weight. However patients being treated with warfarin may have an underlying hypercoagulable state, which may be exacerbated by PCCs. In the absence of available concentrates licensed for warfarin reversal, the option is to use fresh frozen plasma or virus-inactivated plasma at a dose of at least 15 ml/kg body weight, in conjunction with vitamin K as above. The warfarin reversal will be less effective than with concentrate therapy, and larger doses of plasma should be given if possible

B International Normalised Ratio (INR) >8.0; (no bleeding or minor bleeding)

Stop warfarin for 1 or more days; restart when INR <5.0.

Vitamin K, 0.5 - 2.5 mg by mouth if bleeding is present, if age is >70 years, or if there is a history of previous bleeding complications. Oral absorption is rapid. Vitamin K tablets usually contain 5 mg: the I.V. preparation can be given by mouth if necessary (or I.V. if preferred), and the dose repeated the next day if the INR is still too high.

C 3.0 <INR <6.0 (target INR 2.5); 4.0 <INR <6.0 (target INR 3.5): Reduce or stop warfarin. Restart when INR <5.0.

Thrombolytic therapy

Although bleeding is not a common complication of fibrinolytic therapy at normal doses, the risk is not predicted or reduced by laboratory monitoring. If rapid reversal of the fibrinolytic state is necessary because of serious bleeding, fresh frozen plasma will reverse the acquired deficiencies of Factor V and VIIIC; cryoprecipitate will raise a very low fibrinogen level. Antifibrinolytic agents should be used only if there is life-threatening bleeding. They may cause large clots at the site of bleeding, with severe clinical problems. They should not be used in intracranial or renal tract bleeding.

Cardiopulmonary bypass

Cardiopulmonary bypass usually impairs haemostasis due in part to its effect on platelet function. Especially in re-operations or in patients operated on for infective endocarditis, bleeding may be severe. Routine laboratory tests of coagulation do not accurately predict the clinical importance of the haemostatic defect. Platelet transfusion is indicated if there is microvascular bleeding or if the bleeding cannot be corrected surgically after the patient is off bypass and once heparinisation has been reversed with an adequate dose of protamine sulphate. Fresh frozen plasma helps to correct prolonged clotting times and may improve haemostasis, but the routine use of fresh frozen plasma or platelets at the end of bypass does not reduce transfusion requirements.

Aprotinin (Trasylol) can reduce transfusion requirements in specific situations such as bypass surgery in patients with infective endocarditis but routine use is not advised for coronary artery or valve surgery in adults.

Congenital haemostatic disorders

Haemophilia

In Ireland, all patients with Haemophilia A, Haemophilia B (Christmas disease), and von Willebrand's Disease should be registered at the National Haemophilia Centre (children — Tallaght Hospital; adults — St James's Hospital). The majority of these patients will be cared for at these centres for acute bleeds and follow up; patients living within the catchments of the regional haemophilia centres in Cork, Waterford and Galway may be treated and followed up at these centres.

When a patient with haemophilia is seen away from a specialist centre, it is important to get the best help available, quickly. (Table 16)

Table 16: *Points to note in initial care of a bleeding haemophilia patient*

Identification: If the patient is unconscious, check if there is information carried in a wallet, or on a bracelet or medallion. Contact the Haemophilia Centre for advice and inform the local haematologist.

Products for treatment: Coagulation factor concentrates VIIIC and IX respectively are needed for haemophilia A and B. The nearest supply may be in the patient's home provided for home therapy. In a real emergency and if clotting factor concentrates are unavailable, cryoprecipitate is the appropriate treatment for Haemophilia A and fresh frozen plasma is appropriate for Haemophilia B.

Dosage: Factor VIIIC in a dose of 1 iu/kg should give an immediate 2% rise in plasma Factor VIIIC. Factor IX (1 iu/kg) should give an immediate 1% rise in Factor IX level.

Monitoring: Clotting factor levels may be needed to assess response to treatment. Check with your local laboratory that these assays are available.

von Willebrand's Disease (vWD)

The assessment of treatment needs and response is not straightforward and needs measurement of both Factor VIIIC and von Willebrand factor. Some patients can be managed with desmopressin (DDAVP) without the need for any blood product. If clotting factor replacement is needed, a Factor VIIIC concentrate must be chosen that is effective for vWD. Cryoprecipitate was formerly the chosen replacement therapy but should now be used only if a virus-inactivated concentrate is not available.

Every effort must be made to obtain immediate specialist assistance in the management of these patients.

Transfusion in chronic anaemia

Nutritional replacement therapy with iron, vitamin B12 or folic acid or correction of the source of blood loss based on a correct diagnosis should be the treatment in most cases. Chronically anaemic patients are deficient in red cells, but have a normal or increased blood volume. A rapid rise in haemoglobin is rarely required. In rare cases when red cell transfusion is felt to be needed, red cells (rather than whole blood) should be used to minimise the volume given. Patients who are elderly or who have cardiovascular disease or megaloblastic anaemia are most at risk of developing cardiac failure. Therefore red cells should be given slowly (4 hours per unit) at a time when the patient can be observed. A diuretic, such as frusemide should be given if there is felt to be a risk of circulatory overload. *Do not add the diuretic to the blood component pack.*

Transfusion dependent anaemia

Regular red cell transfusion may be required for patients with myelodysplastic syndromes, chronic lymphocytic leukaemia, aplastic anaemia, or malignant infiltration of the bone marrow.

Haemoglobinopathies

Patients with beta thalassaemia major or severe complications of sickle cell disease may need long term red cell support. These patients all require specialist investigation and management. Special precautions must be taken to reduce the risk of developing antibodies to red cells and white cells and the patient should be vaccinated against Hepatitis B and Hepatitis A. Accumulation of iron should be minimised by using a chelating agent (desferrioxamine).

In patients with thalassaemia the aim of a regular red cell transfusion regime is to suppress endogenous red cell production and keep the haemoglobin between 10.5 and 15.0 g/dl. In the other conditions mentioned above, the need for transfusion is determined by the patient's clinical symptoms of anaemia.

If a patient is a potential candidate for bone marrow transplantation, it is important to obtain expert advice <u>before</u> starting transfusion as special selection of blood products will be needed.

Anaemia in chronic renal failure

The treatment of choice is epoietin; to maintain an adequate haemoglobin without the need for regular transfusion. Epoietin should be used according to the local hospital protocol.

Clinical applications of blood products

Bone marrow failure and transplantation

The treatment of malignant haematological disease or solid tumours often causes bone marrow suppression that requires transfusion support with platelets and/or red cells. In these patients, transfusion may be complicated by graft-versus-host-disease (GVHD), cytomegalovirus (CMV) infection, or the development of antibodies to HLA antigens. The last can cause non-haemolytic febrile transfusion reactions and may reduce the clinical effectivness of platelet transfusions. Special precautions can help to minimise these problems.

Red cell transfusion

The principles are given on page 46. Patients should be tested again for red cell antibodies after transfusion if there is a pyrexial reaction to red cells, an unexplained fall in haemoglobin or if the clinical response to red cell transfusion is less than expected.

Platelet transfusion

Platelet transfusions are generally given to patients undergoing myeloablative therapy with or without haematopoietic progenitor cell rescue or with marrow failure from other causes, according to set protocols established and maintained by the haematology services.

Typically, stable, non bleeding patients without fever and without additional haemostatic compromise (such as may be caused for example by co-existing liver disease) are transfused to keep the circulating platelet count above 10×10^9 per litre. This is usually achieved by daily monitoring of the patient and prescibing a dose of platelets when the platelet counts falls close to or below this level. There is sufficient clinical evidence to support this approach, and to avoid unnecessary risk from transfusion by transfusing such patients at higher circulating platelet count levels.

Patients who are febrile, who have clinical evidence of fresh bleeding other than skin purpura, or who have other haemostatic

Clinical applications of blood products

abnormalities should generally be transfused with platelets so as to keep the circulating platelet count above 20 × 10^9 per litre.

Invasive procedures such as lumbar puncture or Hickman line insertion are usually covered with a platelet transfusion.

Clinical response to platelet transfusion

The typical platelet unit or dose supplied by the blood transfusion service will contain at least 2.4 × 10^{11} platelets. A transfusion of platelets should raise the patient's circulating platelet count by about 25 × 10^9 per litre; on the following day the circulating platelet count should ideally still be 10 × 10^9 per litre above the original level. This result is often not achieved, for one or more of a variety of reasons; consistent failure to achieve the desired response is termed refractoriness. Refractoriness may require additional measures if effective therapeutic responses to platelet transfusions are to be achieved.

For practical purposes refractoriness may be considered to be present when there is a failure to raise the next-day platelet count by at least 10 × 10^9 per litre after two consecutive transfusions. When a patient is actively bleeding additional measures may be required after a single platelet transfusion has failed to stop the haemorrhage.

Refractoriness is more often than not due to fever, increased platelet clearance in the presence of drugs, especially antibiotics and antifungals, low grade disseminated intravascular coagulation, or splenomegaly. Alloimmunization to platelet antigens, especially to HLA class 1 antigens on the platelet surface, causes a sizeable minority of cases of clinical refractoriness.

Management of platelet refractoriness

1   In stable patients being treated with prophylactic platelet transfusions: test for antiplatelet antibodies, and transfuse with immunologicallly compatible platelets if antibodies are detected. Such platelets may be either HLA matched or crossmatched. Platelet antibody testing is provided by the Blood Transfusion Centre, which will also provide compatible platelets for

Clinical applications of blood products

transfusion. If antibodies are not detected ensure that no other cause of refractoriness is present. If another cause is present it can reasonably be presumed to be the reason for the poor incremental response to the platelet transfusions. If the cause cannot be removed then further platelet transfusion strategy is empirical. Platelet transfusions can be withheld on the grounds that they are unlikely to be of benefit, or they can be continued on the basis that they are likely to be more of benefit than of harm, and a non incrementing platelet transfusion may not be completely useless. Unfortunately there is no clear evidence in the literature to guide therapy.

2   If transfusion of matched platelets does not result in appropriate increments in the circulating platelet count, then it may be best if the patient does not receive platelet transfusions unless active bleeding is present, the rationale being that there is little or no benefit to be gained from prophylactic platelet transfusions in this setting.

3   If the patient is actively bleeding then almost every practicing clinician would attempt to address the problem by repeated doses of platelets until the haemorrhage stops. There is some low level evidence in the published literature to support this approach.

All patients with aplastic anaemia who may later receive a bone marrow transplant should be given leucocyte depleted red cells and platelets. This is because HLA antibodies can reduce the chance of a successful 'take' of a bone marrow transplant

Graft-versus-host-disease(GvHD): use of gamma-irradiated blood components.

Engraftment of viable lymphocytes transfused with whole blood, red cells or platelets can cause fatal GvHD in patients with severely depressed T-cell immunity e.g. after progenitor cell grafting. *This **must** be prevented by irradiation of all cellular blood components (25-30 Gy). Leucocyte depletion by presently available methods **does not** protect against GvHD.*

Cytomegalovirus(CMV) transmission.

Since CMV infection is an important cause of mortality following transplantation, all bone marrow or peripheral stem cell allograft recipients should receive CMV antibody negative cellular blood products, regardless of the patient's CMV serological status or that of the donor. Fresh frozen plasma and cryoprecipitate have not been shown to transmit CMV. Other patients who should receive CMV negative cellular components include

- CMV negative autograft recipients,
- CMV negative acute leukaemia patients prior to transplant,
- All new patients with haematological malignancy until their CMV status is known,
- HIV positive patients who are CMV negative.
- For some neonatal transfusions and intrauterine transfusion (page 91).

Since CMV is leucocyte-associated, a widely accepted alternative is to use leucocyte depleted cellular components, that have been prepared using validated techniques.

Selection of ABO groups for transfusion of bone marrow allograft recipients.

If the ABO groups of donor and recipient are different the selection of the ABO group of cellular components to be transfused must be discussed with the hospital transfusion department.

Renal transplantation

In the past, 1-2 units of red cells were transfused to patients awaiting transplantation because this led to improved graft survival. Most specialists now consider that immunosuppression with cyclosporin makes this unnecessary. Anaemia is usually treated with recombinant human erythropoietin. If red cells are administered they should be leucocyte depleted to avoid development of HLA antibodies and reduce any risk of CMV infection.

Heart, heart/lung and liver transplantation

Where both donor and recipient are CMV negative, CMV negative red cells and platelets should be used.

Liver transplant patients often have major abnormalities of coagulation and a low platelet count. Local protocols should define the pre-operative and intraoperative use of blood components. Steps often taken to minimise blood usage during surgery include red cell salvage, the use of aprotinin, and continuous infusion of fresh frozen plasma during critical stages of the operation.

Intravenous immunoglobulin for immune cytopenias

Auto-immune thrombocytopenic purpura (AITP):
IVIgG in high doses has a role in the management of some patients but it is not a substitute for standard treatment including steroids and splenectomy. IVIgG produces an increase in the platelet count of varying duration in about 70% of patients but it does not alter the natural course of the disease. IVIgG may be useful:

- To assist management of acute bleeding
- To cover surgery or delivery in patients with AITP if the low platelet count causes risk of haemorrhage

A total dose of 1-2 g/kg divided over 1-5 days is usual in patients with chronic AITP; further occasional doses of 0.4 g/kg may help to maintain an adequate platelet count.

Renal failure has occured in elderly patients following administration of high dose intravenous immunoglobulin. Caution should be exercised in patients with pre-existing renal disease and in the elderly who may be more susceptible.

The use of high doses is associated with an increased rate and severity of adverse reactions, and THE MAXIMUM DAILY DOSE OF 1g/kg MUST NOT BE EXCEEDED. In the elderly, a maximum daily dose of 0.4 g/kg may be safer.

Clinical applications of blood products

Neonatal alloimmune thrombocytopenic purpura (NAITP)
Neonatal thrombocytopenia due to maternal AITP
Post-transfusion purpura

IVIgG has been used in all these conditions with variable results. In NAITP the benefit of high dose IVIgG given to the mother to prevent or reduce the severity of the disorder has not been firmly established. IVIgG given to the neonate is effective in about 50% of NAITP cases and may be used with donor platelets which lack the antigen against which the maternal antibody is directed. In neonatal thrombocytopenia associated with maternal AITP, IV IgG is effective in some cases.

In all these conditions the initial dose should be about 1-2 g/kg. Specialist advice is essential.

Immunoglobulin treatment in antibody deficiency states

Primary hypogammaglobulinaemia

These patients have an inherited deficiency in antibody production. They need life-long replacement therapy to avoid or control the infectious complications of immune deficiency. Because intramuscular IgG is often poorly tolerated due to pain at the injection site (especially in children) it may be impossible to maintain levels of plasma IgG sufficient to prevent recurrent infection. The treatment of choice is regular administration of IVIgG. The standard dose is 0.2 g/kg body weight every 3 weeks but the dose may require to be increased or infusions given more frequently if recurrent infections persist. It is usual to aim to keep the plasma IgG level within the range of normal values. If IMIgG has to be used the conventional dose is 0.025-0.05 g/kg weekly.

Haematological malignancies

Some patients with chronic lymphatic leukaemia or myeloma are unable to make effective antibodies and suffer from recurrent severe infections due to gram positive encapsulated bacteria (e.g. *Strep pneumoniae, H influenzae*) that respond poorly to antibiotics. IVIgG at

Clinical applications of blood products

a dose of 0.2-0.4 g/kg every 3-4 weeks has been shown to reduce the frequency of episodes of these infections.

HIV

Some children with HIV who suffer from recurrent bacterial infections benefit from IVIgG, 0.2 g/kg body weight every 3 weeks. Episodes of infection, antibiotic use and hospitalisation can all be reduced.

Other indications for intravenous immunoglobulin

IVIgG is recommended for routine use in Kawasaki Disease where a dose regimen similar to that used in ITP is effective.

Treatment with IVIgG has been reported to be followed by clinical improvement in many other conditions including neuromuscular disorders that are thought to have an immunological basis. Treatment with IVIgG should generally be part of a clinical trial or may be justfied as a last resort measure.

Immunoglobulin for preventing infection

Normal Human Immunoglobulin (NHIG) and so called 'specific' immunoglobulin products (that contain higher levels of antibody against specific organisms) are used, often together with active immunisation, to protect against infection. A summary of the products and their use is given in Table 17.

Clinical applications of blood products

Table 17: *The use of immunoglobulin preparations for prevention of infection*

Infection	Indications	Preparations	Dose
Hepatitis A	Contacts and travellers requiring short term protection.	**(N.B. vaccine is preferred to NHIG.) Normal Human Immunoglobulin (NHIG)**	see data sheet
	NHIG may interfere with development of immunity from live vaccines. Administer live vaccines, if possible, at least 3 weeks after immunoglobulin.		
Immunoglobulin may interfere with development of active immunity from live virus vaccines. An interval of at least 3 months must elapse after an injection of immunoglobulin before subsequent MMR vaccination is attempted.			
Tetanus	High risk injuries to non-immune subjects	**Tetanus Immunoglobulin**	see data sheet
Use together with active (toxoid) immunisation in tetanus prone wounds in the following: (i) unimmunised subjects, (ii) immunisation history unknown, (iii) over 10 years since last tetanus vaccine. Dose 250 iu but use 500 iu if more than 24 hours have elapsed since injury or if there is heavy contamination of the wound.			
Hepatitis B	Needle stab or mucosal exposure. Sexual exposure	**Hepatitis B Immunoglobulin (HBIG)**	see data sheet
Administer immunoglobulin as soon as possible after exposure, with hepatitis B vaccine.			
Hepatitis B	Newborn babies of high risk mothers	**Hepatitis B Immunoglobulin**	see data sheet
Administer immunoglobulin as soon as possible and with 48 hours after birth, with hepatitis B vaccine.			
Varicella Zoster	Immuno-compromised adult or neonatal contacts.	**Varcella Zoster Immunoglobulin (VZIG)**	see data sheet

Clinical applications of blood products

Table 17–Continued: *The use of immunoglobulin preparations for prevention of infection*

Infection	Indications	Preparations, vial content	Dose
VZIG should be given to:	*Immuno-suppressed patients* who within three months of the contact have been on high-dose steroids (e.g. 2mg/kg/day of prednisolone for more than a week). *Bone marrow transplant recipients.* *Infants up to four weeks after birth:* • whose mothers develop chickenpox (but not zoster) in the period seven days before to one month after delivery • in contact with chickenpox or zoster and whose mothers have no history of chickenpox or who on testing have no antibody • in contact with chickenpox and who are born before 30 weeks of gestation or weighing less than 1kg; they may not possess maternal antibody despite a positive history in the mother. *Pregnant* contacts of chickenpox without a *definite* history of chickenpox should be tested for V-Z antibody before VZIG is given since about two-thirds of women have antibody despite a negative history of chickenpox. Those *without* antibody require VZIG. *HIV positive individuals* with symptoms should be given VZIG after contact with chickenpox unless they are known to have V-Z antibodies.		
Rabies	Bite or mucous membrane exposure to potentially rabid animals	**Human Rabies Immunoglobulin (HBIg) 500 iu**	20 iu/kg

Rabies Immunoglobulin is used with rabies vaccine to provide rapid protection until the vaccine becomes effective. The recommended dose must not be exceeded and should be given at the same time as the vaccine. Half the dose should be infiltrated round the wound and the remainder given by deep intramuscular injection at a site separate from that used for rabies vaccine.

Sources of Supply

NHIG, tetanus immunoglobulin, hepatitis B immunnoglobulin & VZIG are available either through the hospital pharmacy or through the blood bank, depending on local arrangements.

Rabies immunoglobulin is obtained from the UK: CDSC, Central Public Health Laboratory, 61 Colindale Avenue, London NW9 2SE; 0044-181-200 6868.

Transfusion of the newborn infant

Normal values

The blood volume is 80 ml/kg for full term infants and around 100 ml/kg for pre-term infants, depending on gestational age. The normal range of haemoglobin concentration in full-term infants is 14-20 g/dl. Platelet count ranges from 150 to 400 $\times$ 10^9/l. The prothrombin time and thrombin time can be slightly prolonged in full-term infants; more marked prolongation of coagulation times is seen in the pre-term. The level of vitamin K-dependent coagulation factors in the neonate is about 50% of the normal adult value. Fibrinogen and other coagulation factors are in the normal adult range at birth.

Table 18: Normal Ranges for Term and Preterm Infants			
	Term	Preterm (<37 weeks)	Adult
Haemoglobin, g/dl	14-20	12.6-20	13-18
Platelets $\times$ 10^9/l	150-400	150-400	150-400
PT (sec)	12-17	14-22	12-14
APTT (sec)	25-45	35-50	25-40
TT (sec)	12-16	14-18	12-14
Fibrinogen	1.5-3.0	1.5-3.0	1.75-4.5

Normal values for preterm infants depend on gestation.
* These values are illustrative only: results from each laboratory must be related to the laboratory's own normal range.

Small Volume Red Cell transfusions for Neonates

Pre-term infants often require repeated red cell transfusions and are the longest living survivors of blood transfusions. The declining incidence of haemolytic disease of the newborn and improvements in neonatal intensive care have meant that small volume (10–20mls/kg) red cell top-up transfusions are the most frequently administered transfusions to neonates. Every effort must be made to reduce donor exposure in these most vulnerable of transfusion recipients.

Until relatively recently the usual practice was to use blood that had been stored for less than 5–7 days for all transfusions for neonates. This is because the concentration of extracellular K+ rises in stored blood. For this reason babies undergoing massive transfusion e.g. exchange transfusion, should receive blood that is within the first five days of its shelf life. However, hyperkalaemia is not a concern for neonates who are recipients of small volume transfusions of red cells, provided that they are administered slowly over 3–5 hours.

As the actual amount of blood transfused per transfusion episode is small, a unit of blood can be divided into multiple satellite packs of approximately 50mls each (so-called Pedipacks) for repeat transfusions for the same patient. These are available from the Blood Transfusion Service Board. Such units can be ordered for an infant who may require more than one small volume top-up transfusion. This system significantly reduces donor exposure for these patients and should be considered as the product of choice in this setting.

The pedipack format is available for whole blood and for red cell concentrate in additive solution. Red cell concentrates in additive solution are suitable for top up transfusions but not for exchange transfusion or other large volume transfusions in neonates.

Thrombocytopenia in neonates

There is an increased risk of haemorrhage in pre-term infants with moderate thrombocytopenia (50-100 $\times$ 10^9/l) and in full-term infants with platelet counts less than 20-30 $\times$ 10^9/l. The risk is increased if there is sepsis or coagulopathy. One donation of recovered platelets should normally produce an acceptable platelet increment in children under 10 kg bodyweight. If the plasma volume of the platelet concentrate is excessive, the blood bank may be asked to remove plasma to a minimum volume of 10-15 ml per platelet concentrate. Neonates with thrombocytopenic purpura associated with *maternal* autoimmune thombocytopenic purpura (AITP) generally respond well to intravenous immunoglobulin (IVIgG) in a dose of 2 g/kg body weight. Platelet transfusions have no value in prophylaxis of this condition but may be useful if there is bleeding.

Neonatal alloimmune thrombocytopenic purpura (NAITP).

This is a rare, serious condition and specialist advice is required. NAITP is caused by maternal IgG alloantibodies against a paternal platelet-specific alloantigen on the platelets of the fetus/neonate. High dose IVIgG (2 g/kg body weight) given to the neonate is effective in about 50% of cases. However the treatment of choice is to give platelets lacking the paternal alloantigen. In the absence of suitable donor platelets, the mother's platelets may be used. They must be washed to remove the plasma which contains the platelet antibody and <u>must</u> be irradiated.

Haemolytic disease of the newborn (HDN)

What causes HDN?

Haemolytic disease of the newborn is caused by antibodies that are produced by the mother. These antibodies are IgG and can cross the placenta and destroy the baby's red cells.

In the most severe cases of HDN the fetus may die *in utero* or be born with severe anaemia that requires replacement of red cells by exchange transfusion. There may also be severe neurological damage after birth as a result of a high bilirubin level. Effective care of the affected pregnancy and of the newborn requires the skills of a specialist team.

The antibodies that cause HDN are directed against antigens on the baby's red cells that are inherited from the father and are absent in the mother. The mother may develop these antibodies if fetal red blood cells cross the placenta (feto-maternal haemorrhage) during pregnancy or delivery. They may also result from a previous red cell transfusion.

Antibody to the Rh D antigen is the most important cause of HDN. It only occurs in pregnancies in Rh D negative women where the father is Rh D positive. The frequency of HDN due to anti Rh D has been greatly reduced by the prophylactic use of Rh D immunoglobulin and also because family sizes have become smaller.

Although ABO incompatibility between mother and fetus is common, severe HDN due to IgG anti-A and anti-B antibodies is very rare in caucasians but is more common in some black populations. IgG antibodies against other blood group antigens (Rh c, Rh e, Rh C, Rh E, Fy^a, K) occur in about 0.5% of pregnancies. If the fetus is positive for the antigen, the haemolysis can be as severe as in Rh D HDN.

Screening in pregnancy

All pregnant women should have their ABO and Rh D group determined when they book for antenatal care at 12-16 weeks. This identifies Rh D negative mothers; the mother's blood is also tested for any IgG antibodies to red cells that could cause HDN. If these are found, the father's red cell type should also be determined. If he is homozygous for the antigen concerned the fetus will be positive also; if he is heterozygous, there is a 50% chance that the fetus will be positive. If an antibody is detected at booking, it should be monitored throughout the pregnancy in case the level of antibody increases.

If no antibodies are detected at booking, the pregnant woman should have a further antibody check at 28-30 weeks gestation.

If anti-D or other antibodies are found during early pregnancy the level should be checked in accordance with local protocols and taking account of specialist advice.

Prevention of HDN - use of Rh D immunoglobulin ('Anti-D')

This blood product is administered to the Rh D negative mother when there is a risk that fetal Rh D positive red cells may enter her circulation, usually due to a feto-maternal bleed. Anti-D prevents the mother from being immunised and from starting to produce anti Rh D antibodies.

Anti-D should be given as soon as possible after delivery in a dose of at least 120 μgm to a Rh D negative mother who has no Rh D antibodies and who has an Rh D positive infant. The prevention is less effective if anti-D is given later, especially after 72 hours, but even if the correct time for the dose is missed, anti-D should still be given as it may give some protection.

(If rubella vaccine is indicated it should be given, even when anti-D is being given.)

A 120 µgm dose gives protection for feto-maternal haemorrhage of up to 5 ml red cells.

A Kleihauer test (which determines the number of fetal red cells in the mother's circulation) should be done as soon as possible after the baby is delivered when the dose of anti-D is being given. If this shows that the feto-maternal bleed is larger than 4 ml, extra anti-D must be given in a dose of 25 µgm/ml of red cells. These larger bleeds often occur with interventions such as caesarian section, manual removal of the placenta, in twin pregnancy or after abdominal trauma.

Rh D immunoglobulin should also be given to the Rh D negative mother in other situations where she may be exposed to the red cells of her fetus. These situations are stillbirth, abortion (including therapeutic abortion), threatened abortion, ectopic pregnancy, amniocentesis, chorionic villus or fetal blood sampling, external cephalic version, abdominal trauma (eg seat belt injury) and antepartum haemorrhage.

Since mothers with some of these conditions may be seen in general practice or in hospital emergency departments rather than in the obstetric unit, it is important to be alert to the risk of sensitisation and to check the mother's Rh D type. In these situations anti-D immunoglobulin should be given without waiting to determine the probable Rh D type of the father.

For events up to 20 weeks gestation 50 µgm may be given. For later events 120 µgm should be given and a Kleihauer screening test is advised. If there is repeated antepartum haemorrhage in pregnancy, the 120 µgm dose should be repeated every 4-6 weeks. The level of anti-D in the mother's blood can be monitored and should be kept above 0.05 µgm/ml.

Rh D immunoglobulin should also be used to prevent immunisation if for any reason blood components containing Rh D positive red cells (e.g. platelet concentrates), or organs from Rh D positive donors (e.g. bone, kidney) have to be given to a Rh D negative woman of child-bearing age or if Rh D positive blood is inadvertently transfused. The dose is calculated to remove the estimated amount of red cells transfused, as explained above.

Routine antenatal prophylaxis with anti-D. There is evidence that anti-D given in the 3rd trimester (e.g. 120 µgm at 28 and 34 weeks) can further reduce the incidence of sensitisation from the present level of 1.5% to about 0.2%. This practice is being introduced in some units.

Failure to protect. It is important to note that some Rh D negative women still develop anti-D because of failure to give Rh D immunoglobulin as above. Careful attention to the running of the preventive programme is extremely important in avoiding a risk of damage to the mother's future infants.

Management of HDN

Because severe HDN is now rare, women who are at risk of an affected pregnancy should have access to care in a unit that maintains specialist experience through regular management of these problems.

The condition of the fetus must be monitored throughout pregnancy as there may be a need for early delivery or intrauterine transfusion.

Affected neonates may be extremely ill and require specialist intensive therapy.

Chapter 5

Adverse effects
of transfusion

Adverse effects of transfusion

Overview

Blood products, like other treatments, can both benefit and do harm to the patient. Good clinical practice depends on understanding both the benefits that the treatment can provide for each patient and the risks that the treatment may carry for that patient. An essential part of the equation is to take account of the potential benefits and risks for the patient of NOT using a blood product or of using an alternative.

Where does responsibility rest for the various processes and decision elements that make up good transfusion therapy? Essentially, the *manufacturers* must ensure the safety of the product, and *clinicians* must prescribe and use it correctly. There are additional important tasks for which the *hospital transfusion department* usually carries the main responsibility. Table 19 gives a framework for understanding these tasks, and responsibilities, and summarises aspects of safety that are often of concern to patients, parents, or relatives. Tables 26 and 27 provide a summary of all the important adverse effects.

Reporting

In Ireland, adverse effects from transfusion of blood products including red cells, platelets and plasma should be reported to the regional transfusion centre; adverse reactions from plasma products should be reported to the Irish Medicines Board. Addresses and phone/fax numbers are given on page 104. An optional scheme is also in operation in Ireland & the United Kingdom: the Serious Hazards of Transfusion Scheme (SHOT). This scheme collates reports of adverse effects in an anonymised fashion and serves as a very important source for identifying emerging trends in hazards of blood transfusion. Details of the address and fax numbers are given on page 104.

Acute haemolytic or bacterial transfusion reactions

The features are summarised in Table 20.

It is important to monitor the patient for at least the first 15 minutes of the infusion of each unit of blood to detect the earliest clinical evidence of acute reactions due to incompatibility or bacterial contamination.

Incompatible transfused red cells react with the patient's own Anti-A or Anti-B antibodies or other alloantibodies to red cell antigens. This reaction can activate complement and cause disseminated intravascular coagulation (DIC). Infusion of ABO incompatible blood almost always arises from errors in labelling the sample tube or request form or from inadequate checks when a red cell transfusion is being given.

If red cells are by mistake administered to the 'wrong' patient, (i.e. any patient other than the one for whom the red cells were supplied) the chances of ABO incompatibility are about 1 in 3. The reaction is usually most severe if Group A red cells are infused to a Group O patient. In a conscious patient, even a few mls of ABO incompatible blood may cause symptoms within 1 or 2 minutes (Table 20). The patient becomes restless or distressed and may experience pain at the infusion site, flushing, abdominal, flank or substernal pain and breathlessness.

Table 19: Risks of transfusion treatment – an overview

Risk	Impact on Patients or Prospective Patients	Who is Responsible?	Impact on Health Care Providers
Virus infections.	• Fear of receiving blood. • Anxiety. • Need reassurance. • Want alternatives or no blood. • Actual risk is extremely small.	Manufacturer of blood products Prescribing clinician	Very substantial: Pressure for autologous tx, use of expensive drugs such as epoietin. Risk of legal claims. High cost of trying to achieve zero-risk in transfusion.
Accidents e.g. receiving the wrong blood.	• Some patients worry about this. • Actual risk small but ... • Possibly under recognised.	Clinical Team HTD*	Risk of legal claims. Medicolegal risk to individual clinicians.
Bacterial contamination of blood product.	• Patients assume there is no risk. • Very hazardous when it happens. • Actual risk small.	Manufacturer of blood products. Anyone involved in transport and storage of blood products.	Risk mainly to blood product manufacturer and HTD.*
Complications due to red cell antibodies other than antiA + antiB.	• Patients have little knowledge. • Occasionally hazardous • Actual risks due to reactions are very small but ... • Over caution can contribute to delays when transfusion is needed urgently	HTD should detect the antibodies and supply safe blood. Clinical team should keep (and read!) good patient records and warn the hospital transfusion department of possible problems.	
Over transfusion (circulatory overload).	• Patients have little knowledge. • No data about incidence. • Probably under diagnosed and under reported	Clinical team.	
Non febrile haemolytic transfusion reaction	• Regular recipients of red cell and platelets often very aware. • Distressing and unpleasant - not life-threatening. • In at least 2% of transfusions to regular recipients. • Probably under reported	Clinical team. HTD and sometimes blood products manufacture.	Cause of sub optimal patient care, delays for the patient, extra hospital costs.
Not transfusing when it is necessary	• Patients expect this would never happen (apart from Jehovah's Witness). • If there is undue fear of viruses, reluctance to transfuse may put elderly and frail patients at risk.	Clinical Team	

* HTD - Hospital Transfusion Department

In an unconscious or anaesthetised patient, hypotension and uncontrollable bleeding due to DIC may be the only signs of an incompatible transfusion. Oliguria is common and is often followed by acute renal failure.

Table 20:   *Acute haemolytic transfusion reaction – recognition*

Signs and symptoms may occur after only 5-10 ml transfusion of incompatible blood; so observe the patient carefully at the start of the transfusion of each blood unit.

If the patient has any of the following stop the transfusion and investigate.

Symptoms:
- Feeling of apprehension or "something wrong"
- Agitation
- Flushing
- Pain at venepuncture site
- Pain in abdomen, flank or chest

Signs:
- Fever
- Hypotension
- Generalised oozing from wounds or puncture sites
- Haemoglobinaemia
- Haemoglobinuria

Fever is often due to a cause other than acute haemolysis. As an isolated finding, a rise of 1.5C above baseline temperature during transfusion should be investigated.

In unconscious patients only the signs will be evident.

If an acute haemolytic transfusion reaction is suspected, the transfusion must be stopped and urgent steps taken to confirm or exclude this possibility. The differential diagnosis must include infusion of bacterially contaminated blood.

Treatment is described in Table 21.

Table 21: *Acute haemolytic transfusion reaction – management*

Investigation	Treatment
1 Check again that the compatibility label of the blood unit corresponds with the patient's ID band, forms and casenotes. If a mistake is found tell the blood bank urgently since the unit of blood intended for your patient could be transfused to another patient.	1 Stop blood. Replace giving set. Keep IV open with sodium chloride 0.9%. 2 Insert bladder catheter and monitor urine flow. 3 Give fluids to maintain urine output >1.5 ml/kg/hr.
2 Take 40 ml of blood for • Haematology: 5 ml in EDTA tube - FBC, platelet count, direct antiglobulin test (DAT), plasma haemoglobin. 5 ml in dry or EDTA tube depending on local requirements- Repeat compatibility testing. 10 ml in citrated tube - Coagulation screen (prothrombin time, APTT, fibrinogen). • Clinical chemistry: 10 ml for urea or creatinine and electrolytes. • Blood cultures:	4 If urine output <1.5 ml/kg/hr insert CVP line and give fluid challenges. 5 If urine output still <1.5 ml/kg/hr and CVP adequate then give frusemide 80-120 mg. 6 If no diuresis follows frusemide then give mannitol 20% 100ml IV. 7 If urine flow 2 hours after 20% mannitol and frusemide is <1.5 ml/kg/hr. *Seek expert advice - acute renal failure is likely.* 8 If bacterial contamination is suspected treat with broad spectrum intravenous antibiotics. *Seek expert advice.*
3 Return blood pack(s) and giving set to the hospital transfusion department for bacteriology. 4 Check urinalysis. Monitor urine output. 5 Run an ECG and check for evidence of hyperkalaemia. 6 Arrange for repeat coagulation screens and biochemistry 2-4 hourly	9 If patient has hyperkalaemia give 50 ml 50% glucose intravenous solution IV with 10 units of insulin IV. Follow with infusion of 10% glucose IV solution containing 10 units of insulin over 4 hours. Resonium A by nasogastric tube, or rectally, may be needed to control potassium. 10 If disseminated intravascular coagulation (DIC) develops give blood components guided by clinical state and coagulation screen results. 11 If the patient needs further transfusion use rematched blood. There is no increased risk of a second haemolytic reaction.

Reactions due to red cell antibodies other than ABO

Haemolytic reactions can be caused by other red cell antibodies in the recipient's blood, including anti-Rh D, -Rh E, Rh c and K (Kell). Reactions due to anti Rh D are rare since patients generally receive Rh D compatible red cells. Reactions due to these antibodies are usually less severe than those caused by ABO incompatibility since they do not activate complement. Destruction of transfused red cells is mainly in the spleen or liver. The patient may experience fever, nausea and shivering. However, the Jk (Kidd) and Fy (Duffy) antigens do activate complement and can cause severe intravascular haemolysis leading to renal and cardiac failure. Jk antibodies are sometimes very difficult to detect in pretransfusion samples.

A falling Hb or a rise in Hb that is less than expected after transfusion, together with a rise in bilirubin and a positive direct antiglobulin test indicates that the transfused red cells are being destroyed.

Delayed haemolytic transfusion reactions (DHTR)

In patients who have previously been immunised to a red cell antigen during pregnancy or by transfusion, the level of antibody to the blood group antigen may be so low that it cannot be detected in the pretransfusion sample. About 1% of parous women have red cell antibodies that are often undetectable by routine methods before transfusion. After transfusion of red cells bearing that antigen, a rapid, secondary immune response raises the antibody level so that after a few days, transfused red cells bearing the relevant antigen may be rapidly destroyed. The signs of this *delayed haemolytic transfusion reaction* appear 5-10 days after transfusion with fever, falling haemoglobin, jaundice and haemoglobinuria. Clinically significant delayed haemolytic transfusion reactions are rare. No DHTR was found in 530 patients who received almost 2,500 units of blood. Although DHTR is seldom fatal, it can cause further problems for a patient who is already seriously ill.

Non-haemolytic febrile transfusion reactions (NHFTR)

Fever or rigors during red cell or platelet transfusion affect 1-2% of recipients, mainly those who have been immunised to leucocyte antigens by pregnancy or previous transfusion. Antibodies in the patient's plasma react against transfused leucocytes in the blood component. The symptoms are shivering, usually 30-60 minutes after the start of the transfusion, followed by fever. Most reactions can be managed by slowing or stopping the transfusion and giving an antipyretic e.g. paracetamol. (Table 22). It is important to remember that the symptoms could be due to an acute haemolytic transfusion reaction or bacterially contaminated blood. Recurrent, severe reactions in patients who require repeated transfusions of red cells or platelets may be prevented by the use of leucocyte depleted blood components.

Allergic reactions

The symptoms are urticaria and itch within minutes of the transfusion. Symptoms usually subside if the transfusion is slowed and antihistamine is given (e.g. chlorpheniramine 10 mg, by slow intravenous injection or intramuscular injection in patients who are not thrombocytopenic). The transfusion may be continued if there is no progression of symptoms after 30 minutes.

Chlorpheniramine (8 mg orally) should be given before transfusion when a patient has previously experienced repeated allergic reactions.

Table 22: *Prevention of acute transfusion reactions*

- Febrile non haemolytic transfusion reactions (FNHTR).

  If the patient has had 2 or more FNHTR try:

  Paracetamol 1g orally 1 hour before transfusion.
  Paracetamol 1g orally 3 hours after start of red cell transfusion
  Slow transfusion (RCC 4 hours, platelets up to 2 hours)
  Keep the patient warm

  If the above measures fail, try:

  Filtered red cells or platelets*
  Washed cells
  Apheresis platelets

- Allergic reactions.

  If the patient has 1 severe or 2 minor allergic reactions:
  Chlorpheniramine 8 mg orally 30 minutes before transfusion.

- Anaphylaxis.

  Usually unpredictable.

  If the recipient is IgA deficient do not transfuse until you have
  obtained expert advice.

* During 1999 leucocyte depleted red cells and platelets will become
the standard blood components issued to hospitals.

Anaphylaxis

This is a rare but life-threatening complication. Treatment is
summarised in Table 23. It may occasionally be associated with
antibodies against IgA in patients who have extremely low levels of
IgA in their plasma. If this is the suspected cause the patient should
if possible not be transfused. Special products will be needed and
the hospital transfusion department must be consulted.

Table 23: *Treatment of anaphylactic reaction during transfusion*
• Stop the transfusion
• Maintain venous access with 0.9% saline
• Maintain airway and give oxygen
• Give adrenaline 0.5-1mg i.m., repeated every 10 minutes according to blood pressure and pulse until improvement occurs
• Give chlorpheniramine 10-20 mg by slow IV injection
• Give salbutamol by nebuliser
• Get expert advice. If in doubt get the duty anaesthetist.

Transfusion related acute lung injury (TRALI)

This form of acute respiratory distress may be under-recognised. The cause is usually donor plasma that contains antibodies against the patient's leucocytes. Transfusion is followed by a severe reaction with chills, fever, non productive cough and breathlessness. The chest x-ray shows numerous mainly perihilar nodules with infiltration of the lower lung fields. The implicated donors are almost always multiparous women and are found to have antibodies to white cells.

Reporting to the Hospital Transfusion Department and to the Regional Transfusion Centre (page 104) is important so that an implicated donor can be removed from the panel. Treat as for Adult Respiratory Distress Syndrome from other causes.

Fluid overload

When too much fluid is transfused or the transfusion is too rapid, fluid overload can lead to systemic and pulmonary venous engorgement. Pulmonary oedema and acute respiratory failure may follow. Signs may include dyspnoea, tachycardia and hypotension. Standard medical treatment is a diuretic (e.g. frusemide 20mg IV initially) and oxygen. The transfusion should be stopped or slowed. Volume overload is a special risk with 20% albumin solutions.

Patients with chronic anaemia are normovolaemic or hypervolaemic and may have signs of cardiac failure before any fluid is infused. If the patient must be transfused, give red cells rather than whole blood, with diuretic therapy if required. Each unit should be given slowly and the patient closely observed. Restricting transfusion to one unit in each 12 hour period should reduce the risk of LVF.

Late complications of transfusion

Iron Overload

Transfusion dependant patients receiving red cells over a long period become overloaded with iron. Chelation therapy with desferrioxamine is used to minimise accumulation of iron.

Graft vs Host Disease (GvHD)

GvHD is a rare complication of transfusion caused by T-lymphocytes. Immunodeficient patients e.g. recipients of an allogeneic bone marrow transplant and fetuses receiving intrauterine transfusions are at special risk for this disease.

GvHD has also occurred in immunologically normal patients after transfusion of a relative's blood (see page 13). Transfusion associated GvHD is fatal in almost all cases. *Acute* GvHD begins 4-30 days after transfusion with high fever followed by a diffuse erythematous skin rash progressing to erythroderma and desquamation. Gastrointestinal and liver dysfunction occur and pancytopenia is common.

GvHD is prevented by gamma irradiation of cellular blood components to a dose of 25 Gy.

Immunosuppression

Allogeneic blood transfusion alters the recipient's immune system in several ways. Two concerns are:

- Could tumour recurrence rates be increased? Prospective clinical trials have not shown a difference in the prognosis for transfused versus non transfused patients or for recipients of autologous, as opposed to allogeneic blood.
- Does transfusion increase the risk of postoperative infection? Current evidence suggests that transfusion does increase the incidence of postoperative infections in surgical patients, although this remains controversial; also controversial is the suggestion that leucocyte depletion of transfused red blood cells can attenuate this effect.

Post transfusion purpura (PTP)

PTP is a rare but potentially lethal complication of transfusion of red cells or platelets, most often seen in female patients. It is caused by platelet-specific alloantibodies. Typically 5-9 days after transfusion, the patient develops an extremely low platelet count with bleeding. Treatment is with high dose corticosteroids combined with high dose intravenous immunoglobulin. If platelet transfusion is unavoidable, platelets that are compatible with the patient's antibody should be used. Expert advice is needed in managing PTP.

Infections that can be transmitted by transfusion

The perceptions of the risks of transfusion are greatly influenced by HIV transmission that occurred before today's safety testing procedures were available.

Blood donors, like anyone else, can occasionally carry an infectious agent, sometimes for a long period, without having any clinical signs or symptoms. For this reason, the laboratory tests shown in Table 24 are performed on *every* blood donation. No part of the donation can be released until all these tests are known to be clear. Computer systems are used to ensure that no blood with a positive test slips through the net.

There is very good evidence that with the donor selection and testing procedures used in Ireland the risk of infection is extremely small (Table 25). Blood products have become steadily safer over the years as previously unknown viruses have been identified and screening tests for them have been introduced. There has also been continuous improvement in the selection and testing of donors and in manufacturing processes. Inspection, regulation and licensing of the transfusion services by the Irish Medicines Board is an important contributing factor.

Table 24: *Infection Tests – Every donation is checked for:*
● Hepatitis B virus antigen (HBsAg)
● Hepatitis C antibody (HCV Ab)
● HIV1 and 2 antibody (Anti HIV1, Anti HIV2)
● Treponema pallidum antibody
● HTLV I & II antibody

The risk that a blood product may transmit an infectious agent depends on

- Prevalence in the community.
- Combined effectiveness of the processes used to exclude and detect infected donors.
- Viral inactivation.
- Immune status of the recipient.
- Number of individual donors contributing to each dose.

Because all donated units that test positive are discarded, any residual risk of transfusion tramsmitted infection is due to a person donating in the very early phase of infection before antibody is detectable in the donor's plasma—the so-called window period of infection. The risk of this occurring has been calculated for the Republic of Ireland at this time per component transfused as less than 1:3.3 million for HIV, 1:500,000 for HCV and 1:100,000 for HBV (Table 25, [Dr J.O' Riordan, 1998]).

Table 25 gives estimates of the risks of virus transmission.

Table 25: Risks of transfusion-transmitted virus infections in Ireland*
• Plasma fractions
Minimal or zero risk of transmitting HIV, HTLV, HBV or HCV. Should non- enveloped viruses be present in donor plasma they may not be fully inactivated in all current products.
• Blood components
Cellular products are not subjected to a viral inactivation step in production.
HIV Current estimate less than 1 per 3.3 million blood components transfused.
HBV Current estimates approx. 1 per 100,000 components transfused.
HCV Current estimates less than 1 per 500,000 components transfused.
HTLV I/II very remote; no estimate available. the prevalence among Irish donors is extremely low.
*data provided by Dr J O'Riordan, 1998

Hepatitis B

Transmission of Hepatitis B by transfusion is estimated to occur at a rate in the order of 1 in every 100,000 units transfused.

Hepatitis C

Serological tests to detect Hepatitis C virus infection were introduced in 1991 and the tests have been progressively improved since then. The incidence of post transfusion hepatitis has reduced sharply: it is now estimated that less than 1 in 500,000 blood components result in Hepatitis C infection and with the latest, more sensitive screening test the residual risk is further reduced. The infection is usually asymptomatic and revealed only by disturbed liver enzyme tests. About half the affected patients develop chronic hepatitis that can lead after several years to severe liver damage.

Other Hepatitis viruses

Hepatitis A may very occasionally be transmitted by blood products. Other transfusion-transmitted viruses, e.g. hepatitis G, that may be associated with hepatitis have been reported; the clinical significance of these agents remains to be established.

HTLV (I and II)

HTLV I can cause neurological disorders and a form of adult T-cell leukaemia. There is usually a delay of many years between infection and development of illness. It is likely that only a small proportion of those infected become ill. HTLV I is transmissible by the transfusion of cellular blood components. The prevalence of infection is high in some parts of the world, notably Japan and the Caribbean. The link between HTLV II infection and disease is less clear, but infection is found in some intravenous drug users..

CMV

Approximately 30% of Irish blood donors have antibody to CMV, but only a small proportion of antibody positive donations transmit the virus through transfusion. Transfusion transmitted CMV is of proven clinical importance in premature infants weighing less than 1200-1500g who are born to CMV antibody-negative mothers, and in CMV antibody-negative bone marrow allograft recipients who receive CMV sero-negative grafts. Although the risk of clinical CMV infection is much smaller in recipients of autografts, some centres recommend that these patients also should receive CMV negative products, For these patients CMV safe blood components should be given. This is normally done by using donations that do not contain detectable antibody to CMV. An alternative is the use of leucocyte depleted blood components. Fresh frozen plasma and cryoprecipitate do not transmit CMV.

Human parvovirus B19

This non-enveloped virus may not be inactivated in all current plasma fractions. Processes are being developed to do this. There is evidence that HPV B19 infection is associated with bone marrow suppression affecting red cell production in occasional patients.

Treponemal infections

All donations are screened for serological evidence of *Treponema pallidum* infection. A further safeguard is that infectivity of *T. pallidum* declines as blood is stored at 2-6°C.

Chagas disease, caused by *Trypanozoma cruzii* is transmissible by transfusion. This is an important problem in some South and Central American countries where the infection is prevalent, and in donors returning from visits to endemic areas.

Other bacterial infections

Very rarely, bacterial contamination of red cell transfusions occurs. This is a cause of very severe and often lethal transfusion reactions. The estimated incidence is about 1 per million units transfused. Bacteria associated with severe septic reactions to red cell transfusion are usually cold-growing Gram negative species such as *Pseudomonas fluorescens*, an environmental contaminant or *Yersinia enterocolitica*, an organism that may enter a blood donor pack that is collected during an episode of asymptomatic bacteraemia. Skin contaminants such as staphylococci may proliferate in platelet concentrates stored at 20-22°C and this is a factor limiting the safe storage life of platelet concentrates. Bacterial contamination of platelet units may be considerably more common than contamination of red cell units; the severity of reactions to contaminated platelet units may be much less severe, although fatal reactions can occur.

Malaria

Donor selection procedures are designed to exclude potentially infectious individuals from donating red cells for transfusion. Transfusion transmitted malaria occurs with a frequency of about 0.25/million units collected in the USA. This complication has not been reported to date in Ireland.

Creutzfeld-Jakob Disease

Sporadic CJD affects approximately 1 per million of the population. At present there is no evidence to indicate that the prion agent believed responsible for the disease can be spread by blood transfusion, though iatrogenic spread by other means is well recognised. The failure to demonstrate clinical or autopsy evidence of CJD in people with haemophilia suggests that blood products are extremely unlikely to be infectious for CJD.

New variant or variant CJD is considered to be the human form of bovine spongiform encephalitis; it is too early to be confident that it will not be spread by blood transfusion. Considerably more understanding of the biology and epidemiology of this disease is needed to assess the risk of spread by blood or blood products.

Reporting Adverse Effects of Blood Transfusion

Clinical staff observing serious adverse effects of transfusion of blood or blood products should report the event to the Blood Transfusion Service; The Irish Medicines Board must be informed of adverse effects of blood products (contact details on page 104). In addition clinicians are asked to provide details of serious adverse events to the Serious Hazards of Transfusion (SHOT) scheme based in Manchester in the UK (contact details on page 104). SHOT compiles data on serious adverse events that provide valuable information on trends and emerging hazards of transfusion.

Adverse effects of transfusion

Table 26: *Acute complications of transfusion*

Problems	Cause	When? How often?	How dangerous?	Treatment; Avoidance
Acute intravascular haemolysis of transfused red cells.	ABO incompatible transfusion. Group A donor into Group O recipient is worst.	Often during first few ml of infusion. About 1 in 500,000 red cell units transfused.	Mortality 10% due to DIC and acute renal failure. Prevent: use safe documentation and checking systems for blood administration.	*Treat:* Page 82. *Avoid:* Page 29.
Infective shock.	Bacterial contamination of red cells or platelets with e.g. Pseudomonas, Yersinia, Staphylococci.	Usually during infusion of first 100 mls of the contaminated pack. 1 per million red cell units transfused.	Very high mortality	Treat: manage septicaemia. Fluids and intravenous antibiotics e.g. gentamicin plus ceftazidime.
Transfusion Related Acute Lung Injury. Non cardiogenic pulmonary oedema.	Donor plasma has antibody to patient leucocytes.	During or soon after transfusion. *Rare:* Greater risk if large volumes of donor plasma given e.g. whole blood or plasma exchange with donor plasma.	Life-threatening.	*Treat:* Respiratory support, diuretics and high dose steroids. *Avoid:* • Don't transfuse, especially plasma • Donor selection.
Non-Haemolytic Febrile Reactions (NHFTR) to transfusion of platelets and red cells.	Antibodies to transfused white cells. Usually from previous pregnancies or transfusions.	Within an hour or less. About 2% of all transfusion episodes. Mostly in patients who have had several previous transfusions.	Unpleasant, especially if the patient requires regular transfusions.	*Treat:* Paracetamol.* *Avoid:* Use leucocyte depleted cellular components.
Urticaria (allergic reaction).	Patient has antibodies that react with proteins in transfused blood components.		Unpleasant.	*Treat:* Temporarily stop infusion and give chlorpheniramine 10-20 mg iv. *Avoid:* Pre-medicate with chlorpheniramine 8 mg P.O. or 10-20 mg iv before transfusion.

* A simple antipyretic is now thought to be as effective as chlorpheniramine and hydrocortisone. Paracetamol is preferred to aspirin since patients may be thrombocytopenic.

Adverse effects of transfusion

Table 27: *Delayed complications of transfusion*

Problems	Cause	When? How often?	How dangerous?	Treatment; Avoidance
Delayed haemolysis of transfused red cells.	Patient has IgG antibodies to red cell antigens usually Rh c, E. C Kidd - Jka Duffy - Fya Kell - K	5-10 days after red cell transfusion. Less than 1/500 episodes of red cell transfusion.	Reduced survival of transfused red cells so transfusion may be less clinically effective. Consequences of haemolysis can complicate other conditions.	*Treat:* • No treatment for antibodies per se. • Once present, they are a problem for future red cell transfusions so: *Avoid:* • Write prominently in case notes. • Inform the hospital transfusion department when you next request red cells to transfuse the patient. • Good practice in pre-transfusion testing.
Development of antibodies to red cells in the patient's plasma (allo-immunisation)	Transfusion of red cells of a different phenotype from the patient. Also caused by fetal to maternal bleeding during pregnancy and child birth.	Days to weeks after transfusion. Anti RhD will develop in at least 75% of RhD negative patients transfused with a unit of RhD positive cells. Other red cell antigens stimulate antibodies much less frequently. 1-5% of previously transfused or parous patients have red cell antibodies. Antibodies are much more common in female patients.	Dangerous if the patient later receives a red cell transfusion. May cause haemolytic disease of the newborn.	*Treat:* • No treatment for antibodies per se. *Avoid:* *Avoid unnecessary transfusions - especially in premenopausal females.* • *Inform the hospital transfusion department when you next request red cells to transfuse the patient.* • *Good practice in pre-transfusion testing.*

Table 27 Continued: *Delayed complications of transfusion*

Problems	Cause	When? How often?	How dangerous	Treatment; Avoidance
Development of antibodies that react with antigens on white cells or platelets.	Transfusion of blood cells of a different phenotype from the patient. Pregnancy.	About 40% of patients receiving platelet support for more than 2 weeks develop leucocyte and/or platelet antibodies. More likely if patient has a previous pregnancy.	Can cause unpleasant transfusion reactions (NHFTR). Patient antibodies to HLA antigens may contribute to a poor clinical response to platelet transfusion. Page 63. Post transfusion purpura - thrombocytopenia may be profound.	*Treat:* • No treatment for the antibodies per se. • If antibodies reduce clinical response to platelet transfusion, 'compatible' platelets may help (page 63). *Avoid:* • Use effectively leucocyte depleted red cells and platelets.
Iron overload.	One unit of red cells contains 250 mg of iron. It accumulates over a long course of red cell transfusion.	Clinical problems after several years of regular transfusion. Common in long term recipients of frequent red cell transfusion.	Liver damage and other problems are serious.	*Avoid:* • Planned transfusion regime. • Use chelating agent to increase iron excretion.

Chapter 6

Information for patients

Information for patients

Principle

It is good clinical practice to provide adequate information to the patient and to make sure that it is understood. It is recommended that discussion with the patient should include the information in the following outline for a patient information leaflet.

An outline for a patients' guide

This leaflet explains why transfusion of blood is sometimes necessary. You may need transfusion as a planned part of your medical treatment or, if you are having an operation, it may be needed to replace blood loss. Although your consent to operation includes transfusion, it is important that you understand the reasons why blood transfusion might be advisable before you are asked to agree.

Transfusion of blood or individual constituents of it are given to correct abnormalities in your own blood system. This treatment is only advised when these abnormalities cannot be corrected by any other means. Common reasons for giving transfusion include:

1. **Loss of blood**
   An adult has about 10 pints of blood. Loss of small amounts, up to a pint of blood, for example during blood donation, causes no problems. Often loss of larger amounts does not need blood transfusion since other fluids, for example salt and water solution or synthetic substances such as dextrans or gelatin can be used to replace the loss. The loss of a larger amount of blood can be extremely dangerous unless blood or a constituent of blood is given. For some operations, surgeons need to have blood available in case blood loss is more than expected.

2. **Anaemia**
   Anaemia means that the number of red cells in the blood is low. Anaemia often causes tiredness and breathlessness because the

blood cannot carry enough oxygen to where it is needed in the body. There are many different causes for anaemia. Often treatment by drugs or vitamins is effective. If the anaemia does not respond or where rapid recovery is essential, blood transfusion may be the most effective form of treatment.

3. **Bleeding, blood clotting and other problems**
   Sometimes blood loses the ability to clot properly so that bleeding after injury continues for a long time. These problems can often be corrected by giving transfusions of blood products made from blood. These are usually purified clotting substances (for example the substance that people with haemophilia lack) or cells known as platelets that can be extracted from blood donations.

How does your doctor decide what to advise?

Your doctor has to decide when transfusion is the best remedy for the problem you have. Alternative treatment may be available and your doctor will decide whether these can be used instead. Blood transfusion treatment like other forms of treatment including medicines carries a very small risk of harmful effects. Doctors weigh these potential risks very carefully against the benefits of transfusion.

What are the risks?

Over 100,000 transfusions, saving many lives, are given every year in Ireland. The vast majority of these cause no harmful effects. HIV infection (the virus that causes AIDS) is perhaps the best known risk but the chance of this in Ireland is less than one in 3.3 million. This safety is the result of very stringent measures taken by the Blood Transfusion Service to ensure the safety of the blood supply. Hepatitis (jaundice) is another possible complication. Every blood donation is tested for the viruses that cause hepatitis and AIDS.

Clotting factors and other blood protein products undergo virus killing processes that further reduce the risk of transmitted infection.

Other temporary side effects such as feverish reactions may occur. These are minimised by careful selection of blood in the hospital transfusion laboratory. They are usually insignificant compared with the expected benefit of your transfusion.

Can I use my own blood for transfusion instead?

In some circumstances this is possible and sometimes it may be recommended. Your doctor will advise you about whether this would be useful in your own individual circumstances.

The Blood Transfusion Service in Ireland is fortunate in having the support of very large numbers of voluntary blood donors whose only reward is the knowledge that they are giving blood for the benefit of others. The safety of blood transfusion in Ireland is as good as the best in the world.

Sources of information

Further reading

Autologous Transfusion

British Committe for standards in Haematology, Guidelines for Autologous Transfusion I. Pre-operative autologous donation. *Transfusion Med.* 1993, **3,** 307–316.

Cardiac Surgery

Goodnough, L.T., Johnston, M.F.M., Ramsey, G., Sayers, M.H., Eisenstadt, R.S., Anderson, K.C., et el. Guidelines for tranfusion support in patients undergoing coronary artery bypass grafting. *Ann. thorac. Surg.* 1990, **50,** 675–683.

Spence, R.K., Alexander, J.B., DelRossi, A.J., Cernaianu, A.D., Cilley, J., Jr, Pello, M.J., et al. Transfusion guidelines for cardiovascular surgery:lessons learned from operations in Jehovah's Witnesses. *J. vasc., Surg.* 1992, **16,** 825–831.

Collection and Production of Blood Comoponents

UKBTS-NIBSC Liaison Group. *Guidelines for the Blood Transfusion Service,* 2nd Edition. London: HMSO, 1993 (ISBN 0 11 321560 6).

Erythropoietin

MacDougall, I.C., Hutton, R.D., Cavill, I., Coles, G.A., and Williams, J.D. Treating renal anaemia with recombinant human erythropoietin: practical guidelines and a clinical algorithm. *Br. med. J.* 1990, **300,** 655–659.

General

McClelland, D.B.L. (Editor) *Optimal use of donor blood.* Report of a working party set up by the Clinical Resource and Audit group. London: HMSO, 1995 (ISBN 0 7480 2910 9).

Contreras, M. (Editor) *ABC of Transfusion Medicine,* London: British Medical Journal, 1990 (ISBN 0 7279 0288 1).

Wood, K. (Editor) *Standard Haematology Practice/2.* Oxford: Blackwell Science, 1994 (ISBN 0 632 03739 3).

Haemostasis and Thrombosis

British Committee for Standards in Haematology. Guidelines on oral anticoagulation: third edition *Brit. J. Haematol.*, 1998, **101**, 374–387.

Immunoglobulins

Intravenous immunoglobulin: prevention and treatment of disease. NIH Consensus Conference. *JAMA*, 1990, **264**, 3189–3193.

New perspectives on the use of intravenous immunoglobulin. *Clin. exp. Immunol.* 1994, **97**, (Suppl. 1), 1–83.

Recommendations for off-label use of intravenously admistered immunoglobulin preparations. Consensus statement. *JAMA*, 1995, **273**, 1865–1870.

Irradiation of Blood Components

British Committee for Standards in Haematology. Guidelines on gamma irradiation of blood components for the prevention of transfusion-associated graft-versus-host disease. *Transfusion Med.* 1996, 6, 261–271.

Massive Blood Loss

British Committee for Standards in Haematology. Transfusion for massive blood loss, in Roberts, B. (Editor) *Standard Haematology Practice.* Oxford: Blackwell Scientific Publications 1991, pp. 198–206 (ISBN 0 632 02623 5).

Neonatal and Paediatric Transfusion

Sacher, R.A., Luban, N.L.C., and Strauss, R.C. Current practice and guidelines for the transfusion of cellular blood components in the newborn. *Transfusion Med. Rev.* 1989, **3**, 39–54.

British Committee for Standards in Haematology. Guidelines for administration of blood products: transfusion of infants and neonates. *Transfusion Med.* 1994, **4**, 63–69.

Obstetric Haemorrhage

Report on confidential enquiries into maternal deaths in the United Kingdom 1988–1990. London: HMSO, 1994 (ISBN 0 11 321691 2).

Plasma

British Committee for Standards in Haematology. Guidelines for the use of fresh frozen plasma. *Transfusion Med.* 1992, **2**, 57–63.

Platelets

British Committee for Standards in Haematology. Guidelines for platelet transfusions. *Transfusion Med.* 1992, **2,** 311–318.

Procedures and Documentation

British Committee for Standards in Haematology. Guidelines on hospital blood bank documentation and procedures. *Clin. lab. Haematol* 1990, **12,** 209–220.

Red Cells

Perioperative Red Blood Cell Transfusion. Consensus Conference. *JAMA* 1988, **260,** 2700–2703.

Flanagan, P. Red cell transfusions including autologous transfusion. *Prescribers' J.* 1992, **32,** 15–21.

American College of Physicians. Practice strategies for elective red blood cell transfusion. *Ann. intern Med.* 1992, **116,** 403–406.

American Society of Anaesthesiologists Task Force on Blood Component Therapy. Practice Guidelines for Blood Component Therapy. Anaesthesiology 1996, **84,** 732–747.

Welsh, H.G., Meehan, K.R., and Goodnough, L.T. Prudent strategies for elective red blood cell transfusion. *Ann. intern Med.* 1992, **116,** 393–402.

Consensus statement on red cell transfusion. Proceedings of a Consensus Conference held by the Royal College of Physicians of Edinburgh, 9–10 May 1994. *Br. J. Anaesth.* 1994, **73,** 857–859.

Table 28: *Contact details*

	Tel number	Fax number
BTSB HQ & Dublin Centre	01-660 3333	01-6603419
Munster Regional Centre	021-968799	021-313014
National Haemophilia Centre	01-453 7941 ext.2141	01-473 1217
Irish Medicines Board	01-676 4971	01 676 7836
Serious Hazards of Transfusion Office (Dr E Love)	00 44 161 251 4200	00 44 161 251 4331 (confidential fax)

Index

Printed in the United Kingdom for The Stationery Office   J0056994 11/98 C60 10170